Decisions, Decisions

How to Get Off the Fence and Choose What's *Best*—for *You*!

RANDY W. GREEN, PhD

Foreword by Dr. Joseph Riggio

LYONS PRESS
Guilford, Connecticut
An imprint of Globe Pequot Press

To my brothers, Brian and Alan, and my dear friend, Bob Wolfe, all of whom as veterinarians made the exquisite *decision* to dedicate their lives to healing those who dedicate their lives to healing ours . . .

To buy books in quantity for corporate use or incentives, call **(800) 962-0973** or e-mail **premiums@GlobePequot.com**.

Lyons Press is an imprint of Globe Pequot Press

Text Design: Sheryl P. Kober

Library of Congress Cataloging-in-Publication Data
Green, Randy W.
 Decisions, decisions : how to get off the fence and choose what's best for you! Randy W. Green.
  p. cm.
 ISBN 978-0-7627-5745-9
 1. Decision making. I. Title.
 BF448.G74 2010
 153.8'3—dc22
                              2009046734

Printed in the United States of America

10 9 8 7 6 5 4 3 2 1

CONTENTS

FOREWORD

Every once in a while something old and extremely valuable is rediscovered. When this occurs the Wheel of Knowledge undergoes another revolution and what emerges is both the same and radically renewed, and therefore different. Those who are unfamiliar with the origins of this ancient wisdom will perceive it as something new, and often that's enough to capture their interest. Those who are familiar with the ancient wisdom will recognize it for what it is and be attracted because they realize the value of what's on offer. What Dr. Randy Green shares in this book is an example of the turning of the Wheel of Knowledge, something profoundly important and supremely relevant to our times. In the early 1970s two explorers of human experience, Richard Bandler and John Grinder, formulated a technology of excellence they called Neuro-Linguistic Programming. Their work has been praised as the most important work in advancing the understanding of applied psychology in the last decades of the twentieth century. The essence of what they uncovered follows:

1. Each individual experiences the events of his or her life uniquely.

2. These events are coded in specific patterns that are accessible and malleable.

3. By attending to the form of the way events are coded instead of what is customarily attended to, the content

of those events, one's experience can be programmed or guided to produce intended, useful, and lasting results.

These ideas are truly amazing with regard to their impact on human performance and the ability to build experiences in relation to creating desired outcomes. From applications as diverse as therapy, education, business, and sports, as well as others, Neuro-Linguistic Programming or NLP has become a leading-edge technology of producing excellence with individuals and with groups of people.

Roye Fraser, a student of NLP, took a radical approach to working with the technology of NLP that was based in a purely positive direction. His underlying assumption is that each individual has an innate template of excellence for living his or her life, a Success Blueprint of sorts. Roye called this template the Generative Imprint, and pursuing the understanding of the impact of this imprint became his life's work. His legacy is clear in that the material he developed is truly revolutionary in its ability to create positive change in the lives of people who encounter it. You'll learn much more about Roye's model in these pages.

At its simplest, what Roye realized and codified was that people make a fundamental choice in their lives, either to live from a positive orientation that is focused on possibilities or a negative orientation that is mostly focused on limitations. When the choice to organize in relation to possibilities is made, an individual shifts his or her entire being—thoughts, feelings, behavior, and the expression of those events held within the body—in a specific way to generate a pervasive sense of well-being. This fundamental choice determines how we experience everything; either life is full of possibilities, or it is full of limitations.

I met Roye in 1987 and became a student and apprentice to the work he was offering. From that intensive learning experience I developed the Mythogenic Self Process model. I began teaching this work in 1994 and have delivered programs based on this model in more than thirty countries since then. In 2004 I was introduced to Dr. Randy Green by a student of mine, Devon White. Randy brought a tremendous thirst for learning and a significant clinical background to the work we've done together since that time.

As you read through this account, which is considered from the point of view of possibility, you'll find that Randy offers what may be a totally different and unique approach to decision-making than you've ever come across before. Most books on decision-making take the position that decision-making is a mental activity dependent upon analysis of the information presented. Usually this analysis involves carefully considering the data and balancing the risks and rewards—the benefits and the costs, the upsides and the downsides—yet all of this is really just a way of formalizing an act of speculation, i.e., fancy guesswork.

Instead of that kind of detailed analytical modeling, what we can consider a cognitive approach to decision making, what you'll find here is a radically different approach based on body awareness. Dr. Green will introduce you to a way of becoming sensitive to the most subtle signals in your body that indicate a response to the information present in terms of "yes" or "no." Using these signals as the basis of decision-making creates a remarkably trustworthy means of making significant decisions, especially when there is little data available from which to make the necessary decisions in a particular moment.

The steps we need to take to create the necessary sensitivity to these body-based signals, which are the basis of the form of decision-making that Dr. Green will be introducing you to in this book, come directly from the legacy of the work of Roye Fraser and the Generative Imprint model. What is most significant about this work is how it goes well beyond decision-making. To develop the necessary sensitivity to the body-based signals, it is first necessary to become sensitive to how you are at your best, how you are when you are organized in relation to possibility.

As you experience the material that Randy introduces here, you'll find yourself learning things about yourself that you've probably never imagined. The brilliance of the model that Randy shares with you is how it so naturally grafts together your access to an extraordinarily positive way of being in the world and the remarkable decision-making that flows from it. What's effective is the method Randy uses to present the material: providing numerous case studies and stories of actual clients he's worked with using this model. Instead of a dry and distant description of the decision-making model, Randy opens it up to you through the actual, lived experiences of people who have benefited from applying it in their own lives.

I've been working with this material for more than twenty years, and as the architect and designer of the Mythogenic Self Process model, I've had the opportunity to work with thousands of clients including senior executives of multinational corporations, retired professionals, educators, students, parents, and others. In every case what I've found is that if someone has the interest, he or she can and does learn how to apply this model, and often the result is not just that he or she learns a powerful decision-making tool, but that his or her life changes in ways that are significantly positive and beneficial.

It is common today to hear about positive psychology, and there seems to be a new book released every week about happiness—what it is, how to get it for yourself, the importance of it in every aspect of life—as though being positive or the pursuit of happiness is a new and novel idea. However, the work that Roye began more than three decades ago was founded in the simple idea that the outcomes you attain operating from a positive position are superior to those you can attain in any other way. Of course, it also makes perfect sense to even the casual reader that coming from a positive body position is more likely to lead to happiness than operating from any other position.

What Dr. Green most amply demonstrates is that with sufficient skill this model can be applied to almost any situation you find yourself in that requires you to make the best decision possible in the moment. In the work I've developed and use with my own clients around the world, I refer to this as making high-quality decisions, decisions that maximize positive consequences and minimize negative consequences. This process has been applied with great success by individuals and within organizations around the world. Now you have in your hands the opportunity to learn and use this same remarkable decision-making process in your own life.

Get ready to experience a most enjoyable reading experience, knowing that when you arrive on the other side of this book you will have learned something about how to make decisions and live a life you may have only dreamed of before. With these final words I turn you over to the most capable hands of a wonderful student of the material you are about to encounter and a polished professional who will guide you through the next steps on this journey called life.

Dr. Joseph Riggio
Princeton, NJ
November 2009

INTRODUCTION

When I was eight years old, I finger-trained a canary. To the surprise and delight of my family, I could get this customarily timid bird to sit on my finger without trembling, fluttering its wings, or biting me. From this event was spawned the idea that I should become a veterinarian. It sounded more like a decision coming from my parents—a decision born out of love, admiration, and respect for my "talents," but nevertheless, a *decision.*

In the years that followed, my parents told people that their son, Randy, was going to become a vet "because he finger-trained a canary when he was eight and therefore had a way with animals." Mind you, we had no other pets in the house but birds during those years.

When someone would ask me, "So, Rand, what do you want to be when you grow up?", I would respond, "A veterinarian."

"Oh really? And why is that?"

"I finger-trained a canary when I was eight." It seemed to make sense at the time. What did I know?

Soon enough, it was time to actually answer that question, and in the process, to make a choice. First, as my senior year of high school approached, I was encouraged to apply to universities that contained veterinary colleges. Second, since a career as a veterinarian appeared to be my destiny, I thought it would be interesting to get my hands dirty—literally—by working for a vet. Also, I reasoned, it would increase my chances of being accepted into a pre-vet college program.

So, the summer between my junior and senior years in high school, I applied for a job with a veterinarian, Dr. Weiss. He asked me why I wanted to become a vet. "Well, Dr. Weiss, I finger-trained a canary when I was eight . . ."

He had me start in the kennel area. This was a long, narrow section of his practice designated for exercising the animals and allowing them to relieve themselves. It consisted of a large, rectangular cement pan pitched from all directions toward a center drain and bordered at its perimeter by low, curb-like cement walls. My job was to sweep it clean and hose it down. After an hour, I failed to see how having trained a canary translated into an aptitude for sweeping excrement.

I was rescued from this menial task later that day by a request from Dr. Weiss: "Randy, would you please get Brutus out of cage five and bring him to me; he's due for his distemper shot."

Brutus was a 120-pound German shepherd with very sharp teeth and hot breath. I weighed about the same as he did, but I wasn't as strong and didn't need a distemper shot, so I wasn't nearly as determined as he was at that moment.

I approached cage five and thought about opening the latch that separated us. Brutus looked at me and showed me his teeth, as if to say, "Go ahead, sucker, open the cage. Stick your hand in and come and get me so I can get that shot." A wry smile seemed to come across Brutus's face.

"Dr. Weiss, Brutus seems to want to stay put for now. Can he get his shot later?"

What happened next resonated throughout my body in such a fashion as to cause me to immediately change my mind about becoming a vet. Dr. Weiss approached Brutus, grabbed him by the scruff of the neck, and dragged him out of the cage. Brutus whined as he submitted to being injected.

"Dr. Weiss, what if he had bitten you?" I asked.

"You have to show an animal who's boss—you can't let him intimidate you," he replied. "Animals can smell fear."

"Yeah," I said, "he was probably choking on mine! But have you ever been bitten in the process?"

"Oh, sure," Dr. Weiss said. "It happens from time to time."

My job at Weiss Animal Hospital lasted one day. In my mind, I couldn't reconcile "from time to time I may lose a finger" with "I finger-trained a canary and should become a veterinarian."

Later, my oldest and best friend Bob, who attended Michigan State University with me and did become a veterinarian, bought Dr. Weiss's practice. He has been bitten several times—by cats as well as dogs. Both of my brothers also became veterinarians and now own animal hospitals. When my brother Alan was working for a vet prior to completing his training, a German shepherd bit his eyelid, and he needed emergency surgery to repair a tear duct. He has been bitten several other times as well. My brother Brian has experienced this occupational hazard with several bite episodes of his own. In fact, his resolve to help animals transcended the fear of being bitten, as he once even had a tiger on his exam table! (Fortunately, it was unconscious and missed the opportunity for a hefty snack.) Although I was the first to decide on a veterinary career, I ultimately changed my mind, while Bob and both of my brothers stuck with their choices and immersed themselves in this profession.

Not having really researched what was required to become a veterinarian, nor what it entailed to function as one, and somewhat disillusioned by my experience at Dr. Weiss's hospital, I initially felt stuck. For most of my life I'd heard that I ought to become a vet, but now I just felt confused. I decided to reevaluate my career choice, which seemed more an outgrowth of the beliefs, encouragement, and feedback I had received from others than what I had deemed the right thing for me to be doing. I wasn't sure at this point how I would know when I chose the right thing, but I knew it had to be something other than becoming a vet. In selecting a new choice, I was moving away from the previous one.

Entering college, I decided to pursue a career in dentistry. But after my sophomore year at Michigan State, it occurred to me that I didn't enjoy looking inside my own mouth, much less the mouths of others. I gagged at the thought of doing that for the rest of my life, and experienced a tightening in my chest as if someone were taking my breath away. Once again, something about this decision was drastically wrong. Despite having done some research this time into what schooling was necessary and how a dentist functions, after two years of pre-dentistry course work, I had a strong feeling in my body that this was also the wrong decision.

And so I rolled the dice again with a new criterion in mind: I wanted to make a choice that I could actually embody in a positive way—to do something that I would somehow recognize as the right thing for me to be doing. When I was exposed to the field of psychology, I experienced something new. Rather than making a decision based on what something was *not*—which I did when I moved from veterinary medicine to dentistry—this time, I made a decision based on how I would function in the world as a psychologist. And for the first time, I felt throughout my being that this choice reflected who I truly am. I can recall a certain stillness—a coming to rest—within my gut after I'd made this decision, followed by some other physical sensations, indicating just how meaningful a career this would be for me.

In the process of becoming a New York State–Licensed Psychologist, I have made hundreds of decisions directly relating to this career path—decisions that frequently began with some indecision, usually involving the question, "Why can't I decide?"

Why do some people labor over life decisions that others seem to handle with ease? For years after that sequence of events at Dr. Weiss's practice, I wondered why my friend Bob and both of my brothers, Brian and Alan, seemed to have had little difficulty deciding to become vets. Little did I know that each of them in turn wondered why I had decided to become a psychologist, a profession that would require me to listen to the turmoil and distress of hundreds of people over a span of many years.

Not ever having obtained a satisfactory answer to this question of *Why?*, it became apparent to me during the course of my professional development as a psychologist that a better question regarding the decision-making process might be *How?*

How does a person create the possibilities in his or her mind from which to choose?

How do people become stuck by not being able to decide?

What are some of the factors of decision-making that keep them stuck?

And, most important, how can people free themselves from those difficulties and make decisions that are self-enhancing?

MY PROFESSIONAL EVOLUTION

As I progressed from studying behavioral psychology and practicing in the private sector using that model, to studying and earning my certification at the master practitioner level in the

Neuro-Linguistic Programming™ (NLP) model, developed by doctors Richard Bandler and John Grinder, I began asking a slightly different question in relation to decision-making: How does a person create the tiny internal experiences—pictures, sounds, feelings—that lead to a particular set of external behaviors? And how can they modify these internal events, often called perceptions or thoughts, in ways that lead to making more useful decisions? NLP is a model that offers a set of tools for creating and tracking the internal sensory experiences that lead to making desirable and useful decisions.

A person may make the same self-defeating decision in the presence of certain events over and over again and then berate himself after the fact—a little like deciding to close the barn door in his mind after all those little evil "decision horses" have already escaped.

A Sweet Choice

Susan B., an obese woman, decided that she wanted to lose weight. She had a thing for hazelnut chocolate cake, which she frequently created as a pastry chef teaching at the Culinary Institute of America in Hyde Park, New York. Listening to her descriptions was enough to make your mouth water.

As she described a hazelnut chocolate cake she had just baked, she ran a lot of internal dialogue in her mind about the scent and taste of it, leading to deep kinesthetic breathing, a feeling deep within her abdomen, followed by a strong motivation to go out and immediately create another one!

Using NLP, I redirected her internal pictures away from the bakery to (what is now called) Mike Arteaga's Health and Fitness Center, a gym that was located near the Culinary Institute. She would be directed to see herself working out, and then, to step into those pictures and actually "be" in the workout, generating a picture of the outcome she'd requested when we first met: a really toned body. I then had her comment on how she expected to feel when she purchased a bathing suit, and when she walked the beaches of the Jersey Shore and noticed heads turning.

Initially, Susan learned how the internal experiences she created had led her to make the overt choices that sustained her obesity. Then she learned how she could alter those internal experiences—pictures, sounds, and feelings—and make better choices. She was further introduced to how she holds choices in her body, both good ones and poor ones, and how she can instigate shifts in the way she holds experiences to produce more useful and lasting outcomes.

Two months after she'd left counseling, Susan called to report that she'd lost twenty pounds, she was going to the gym three times a week, and she'd created some recipes for restricted-calorie desserts that she was using in her teaching. In the process of doing so, Susan had shifted from making decisions that sustained an undesirable way of being (i.e., obese) to making decisions that were based on what was truly in her best interests.

The Mythogenic Self Process

In recent years, my professional orientation has evolved, and I now use another model of human behavior that differs from others I have used—including NLP—in some important ways:

- The foundation or *ground* of any experience is the fact that the way we behave—including how we make decisions—first and foremost shows up in our bodies and is held in the neuromusculature in very specific ways. This consists of tightened muscles in various parts of the body; breathing changes (such as from high in the chest or low, abdominally); postural shifts; gestures with head, hands, and body; and eye movements. This is collectively referred to as the *somatic form*. This form shifts for each and every experience or decision that occurs during the course of our day. Notice how this differs from conventional approaches to decision-making that focus on the "mind"—what you think and feel.

- The framework of this model is highly positive. Rather than beginning with fixing problems, as NLP and almost every other model in psychology does, we start from what people are like when they are working perfectly—when they are at their best.

- It is from this place that people will make decisions in their own best interests. This model emphasizes learning to make powerful, positive decisions by design, with confidence and ease.

This extraordinary model, developed by Dr. Joseph Riggio, is known as the Mythogenic Self™ Process.

Perhaps you are stuck in an unfulfilling relationship and don't have the courage or tools to decide to leave. You might believe that your current vocation is not your avocation—that what you now do for a living falls short of your aspirations and talents. And despite being there for years without having achieved established goals, you can't shift gears; you're stuck in neutral. Or maybe you just find it difficult to make decisions that involve gifts, activities, wardrobe, and entertainment, and even whether or not to visit family.

If you have been reactionary—that is, accepting of anything that comes your way instead of operating proactively and taking the initiative to make life-enhancing, smart decisions—then you will find what follows to be truly enlightening.

WHAT YOU CAN EXPECT

If you have difficulty making decisions, this book will lead you to a place where decisions can happen with "intentionality"; that is, purposefully, with a sense of comfort and confidence. In the process, you will be led on a journey through some unexplored territory in the world of decision-making, in three parts:

- In Part 1, we will identify scenarios that typically lead you to indecisiveness. We will explore the various contexts in your life that require decision-making—from small everyday challenges to choices that affect your health; carry large consequences, such as major purchases; or involve ramifications for other people who may be affected.

- Part 2 will introduce the premise that becoming stuck is an *acquired skill*. We will explore several possible avenues to explain how you may have gotten to this point.

- And finally, in Part 3, you will be introduced to some revolutionary suggestions for what you can do to become more proficient in making decisions anytime, anywhere, with anyone—or even with no one at all, regardless of circumstances.

Cases and Points

During the past three decades, I have counseled adults, adolescents, and children who were often unable to make decisions. Some had to do with relationship issues, such as whether or not to marry, or whether to remain married or get a divorce. For others, it was whether or not to even ask someone for a date. Then there were those issues of a professional nature: "I can't decide whether or not to ask for a raise"; or "I don't think I can give a presentation in front of people even though it's part of my job requirement. I think I'll make a fool of myself."

Still others have been within the realm of parental guidance. "Should I take away my son's TV and computer?" "I can't get my daughter to do her chores." "How do I decide if I can trust that my son is being honest with me about refraining from drugs and cigarettes?" "How do I get my daughter to *want* to do her homework?"

And then there have been those who have sought counsel for emotionally laden decisions affected by anxiety, depression, and phobias. "How can I stop being depressed when nothing good is happening to me?" "How do you decide to stop being anxious— you can't just turn it off like a faucet . . . can you?" "I can't leave my house. Just stepping out to get the mail takes my breath away!" "I come right to the beginning of that bridge and I freeze. I mean, just the thought of going across makes me hyperventilate!"

Bridge Work

I once had a bridge-phobic client in Poughkeepsie, and I convinced him to take a ride with me around town in my convertible, a 1980 Triumph TR-8, the only Triumph ever made with a V8 engine. He liked "muscle cars," and this was, at the time, England's answer to the Camaro. The secret to convincing him was simply being genuine: Every pore in my body indicated that I believed his going for a ride with me was in his best interests. "This is a whisper jet that never leaves the ground," I told him. He smiled and got in.

I revved up the five-speed transmission. The engine roared, and then I turned toward the approach to the Mid-Hudson Bridge. Inhaling, his jaw dropped, and suddenly, this 200-pound man said, "No. I can't go across. Stop. I've tried many times to decide to go over this bridge, but I can't do it! Stop, or I swear I'll jump!" He actually got up on his knees and faced toward the rear of the car. I told him very calmly, "Sit down, or we'll both end up in the Hudson!" He turned white, looked at me, closed his eyes, and sat down. I then asked him to describe what it was like to drive the muscle car of his dreams. He offered what could almost pass as a smile through the panic-stricken expression on his face.

We made it across to Highland. He looked at me in disbelief. I had him check his pulse, and then he shared his own muscle car story. His entire body—face, shoulders, abdomen, and even legs—shifted position. We then went back the way we'd come.

Call it by-the-seat-of-your-pants therapy. Instead of spending months attempting to have him develop insight into his phobia, or systematically desensitizing him to gradual degrees of imagined anxiety-provoking scenes, I chose the real McCoy. That forced an instant decision that changed his life. After that day, he was able to cross bridges with considerably less anxiety.

What I submit to you is that the first place in which this decision manifested was his *body,* not his mind (as in his emotions or thoughts). This idea will become clearer as you read on.

The choice to cross bridges more comfortably that he made subsequently is an example of what we refer to as *exquisite* decisions, those in which body language is in total alignment with thoughts and behaviors. In Part 3, you will learn more about how to make exquisite decisions by beginning from an actual position within your body that represents who you know yourself to be *at your best* and from there, placing your attention where you most want it to go. You will discover that all experiences—thoughts, feelings, and actions—are first represented through the somatic form. This means that the actual position you hold in your body leads to the thoughts, feelings, and actions—including decisions—that are specific to that body form.

When you operate at your *best,* your being radiates outward into the world through the somatic form you hold, expressed by your gait, musculature, posture, breathing, and voice inflection. This affects your behavior in a highly positive fashion, which is not only noticeable to you, but which also begins to infect the world around you. Attracting other people toward the field of possibility that this way of being represents, you are able to make decisions confidently, calmly, and decisively.

So go ahead, be comfortable, and prepare yourself to reminisce, laugh, and learn to get off the fence, and in the process, to make some exquisite decisions of your own.

PART ONE
WHERE DO WE GO WRONG?

CHAPTER 1

WHY ASK "WHY" QUESTIONS?

Successful people ask better questions, and as a result, they get better answers.

ANTHONY ROBBINS

"Why can't I decide whether or not to change careers?"

"Why can't I decide what to buy my husband for his birthday?"

"Brett, why can't you just decide to clean your room when I ask?"

"Why can't I decide what to wear to this stupid reception?"

"Why can't I decide whether or not to ask my boss for a raise?"

"Hmm . . . so many good choices; why can't I decide what to order for dinner?"

Sound familiar? Undoubtedly, many of you have asked these or similar "Why" questions. In fact, because of the manner in which these questions are phrased, you may even recall a time when you felt frustrated by the confusing, unrelated, or unsatisfactory answer that likely followed your question. When "Why?" is the question, "Because" can be the only answer—if you get an answer at all:

"Because . . . I don't know."

"Because I'm afraid I'll choose the wrong thing."

"Because . . . I didn't feel like it."

"Just because."

Or if you had a mother who was skilled at avoiding and redirecting conversation when faced with questions she didn't want to answer, " 'Y' is a crooked letter."

"WHY" QUESTIONS OFFER LITTLE BANG FOR THE BUCK

A "Why" question is highly inefficient, yet it is often the only question people ask themselves—or others—as a way of eliciting their own set of rules that keep them stuck and unable to decide something.

A "Why" question usually leads to a justification of someone's failure to do something, a defense for having tried in vain to select a particular choice that would represent a decision. In other words, at best you get a kind of avoidance response—a "buck." What is presupposed by the "Why" question is that a successful decision—a "bang"—should have taken place.

The reason a "Why" is inefficient is because asking it will rarely generate either the desired outcome—a decision—or a reason for the lack thereof. Instead, "Why can't I?" immediately sets up an undesirable scenario: You (or another recipient) may feel angry, frustrated, embarrassed, confused, or disappointed, and offer an emotionally charged response in defense of not being able to decide.

"Because . . . well, there's just not enough time," or "Because I'm overwhelmed—too many choices!" Worse yet, "Because . . . I don't know." Or the ultimate reflection of "I don't know": dead silence in response to your "Why" question.

There is a wealth of information suggesting why people have difficulty making decisions, much of which is tautological: They can't decide because they have become capable of *not* making decisions.

Now, I ask you: Did that "Because" response satisfy your "Why" question about the difficulty people have making decisions? A tautology can really make you spin your wheels, can't it?

Clearly, the quality of information gleaned from a "Why" question is quite poor, and asking this type of question is an inefficient way to discover useful suggestions or conclusions.

In my profession of psychology, the answer—"Because"—to why you can't decide often refers to diagnoses about past events or behavior. These labels include things like bipolar disorder, dependent personality disorder, and attention deficit disorder; or, less formally, this information can take a more vernacular form, with labels like low self-esteem, lack of confidence, poor upbringing, poor genes, anxiety—maybe even the "Rodney Dangerfield Syndrome" (I get no respect!). Whatever the attribute, basically what is implied is that people can't decide because something inside of them prevents decisions from happening.

What makes a tautology useless—and even harmful in some instances—apart from the fact that you are going in a circle, stating the same thing twice in different ways, is that the very thing implied here as internal "damage" to your psyche, the cause for indecision, cannot be disproven. Just like you can't decide it's true, you also can't decide it's false!

When you respond to "Why can't I decide?" by telling yourself that it is likely a function of poor upbringing, low self-esteem, or the fact that as a child you were criticized for acting too dependent, there is nothing to suggest the contrary. That is, when is this not true? Under what circumstances would you conclude that your difficulty in deciding is not in any way, shape, or form related to childhood diagnoses and behavioral characteristics?

Worst of all, you are left believing that there is no hope for you to learn how to decide in any particular situation, because not deciding is purportedly related to some presumed process that either occurred previously or is currently operating inside of you, and that you simply cannot change.

By illustration, how can you know for sure that your inability to decide whether or not to wear a particular type of outfit—formal or informal—to a particularly important social event stems from your poor feelings about yourself when you were twelve? On the contrary, how could you prove that your alleged low self-esteem at age twelve has nothing to do with your present quandary over dressing for an occasion? The only thing you *do* know for sure is that you are not certain whether or not to wear that outfit. The "Why" question seems out of the question!

Children are supposed to clean their rooms just like they are supposed to brush their teeth, eat their veggies, and get up on time to catch the school bus. These are all decisions, albeit decisions that are frequently made for them by their loving parents, who want their children to embrace the same decision-making strategies that they use. For example, as a parent, you walk by your room and notice things on the floor that belong in the closet. So you suddenly feel the overwhelming motivation to hang them up. Makes sense, right? When the criteria children use to make decisions differ from those of their parents, the first thing asked by a parent is . . . you guessed it: "Why?"

When a mother asks her son Jimmy, "Why didn't you clean your room this morning, and why are those cartoons still on?", she may get a temper tantrum laced with excuses, or she may get no response at all. But as her question is inefficient (meaning, her concern is getting Jimmy to clean his room, not to find out "why" it hasn't been done), she inadvertently allows him to escape by justifying himself, thereby encouraging sloppiness. The mother gets very little "bang" for her "Why" question. *Some children learn to be sloppy, and learn well.*

In a similar way, asking yourself "Why can't I decide?", and then turning inward and postulating guesses based on a time that no longer exists—the past—is a way of buying poor-quality information—*poor* in that it doesn't lead out of the bind you have created; it doesn't suggest a way that you can now decide. This is the type of reasoning that keeps people recycling useless questions that keep them stuck, seemingly incapable of deciding, with no apparent way out. Is it any wonder that indecision is often accompanied by indigestion?

QUESTIONS THAT BUY BETTER-QUALITY INFORMATION

Questions directionalize thought; they help you determine where you are going with an idea. This is vital when it comes to the question of whether or not you are able to decide something. When asking a question pursuant to making a decision, consider what information it will buy you. A well-formed question will elicit more highly valued information than an inefficient one. It's important to pay attention to the types of information you are requesting. Simply asking, "Why?" or "Why can't . . . ?" yields little insight into what specific criteria need to be present in order to render a useful decision.

Throughout this book I will emphasize that when it comes to making decisions, the more highly valued information you are able to gather, the greater will be your likelihood of making a good decision.

"How, specifically, do you know that your current career is not satisfying?"

"Brett, when during the next hour can I expect that this room will be clean?"

"What do I imagine I could get my husband for his birthday that will lead to that little-boy look of wonderment that I just love?"

QUESTIONING LOGIC

Underlying "Why" questions is often the idea that in order to decide something, it needs to make sense in a cognitive sort of way; it needs to be logical. But often, things that would otherwise be logical are not what they seem, which is one more reason "Why" questions are inefficient.

To Ski or Not to Ski . . .

Steven, an attorney and friend of mine from Boston who owned the building in which I rented an office, was addicted to skiing—and the Red Sox. He had fallen while skiing and his right leg was in a cast that began at his pelvis and descended to his foot.

"It's nothing. I was hot-dogging and got a little out of control. Don't worry, I'll be all right," he told me.

I was speechless. He continued, "Ahhh, Rand . . . I had such a great time. You know, you really have to take up skiing."

I thought he might have also injured his head and quite possibly needed a few sessions with me.

"No, Randy. Don't judge skiing by what happened to me. I've been skiing most of my life. I just got a little out of control.

That won't happen to you because you're a beginner. Trust me," Steve said. "Make a reservation at this place just north of Montreal. They're the best ski school around. You'll have a blast." Steve smiled with a faraway look.

I was both stirred and puzzled by this conversation. Why would I want to risk breaking my leg skiing? Looking at Steve, I reasoned that skiing was clearly dangerous—and yet exhilarating.

Steve had apparently decided to ski again from a very comfortable, calm place deep within him; a place that in all likelihood reflected who he was at his best. His ebullience was magnetic and seemed to generate both approach and avoidance in me.

I couldn't decide what to do. I needed a better question than "Why?"—one that would lead to feeling secure in deciding to learn this sport. The question became "What?", and the answer was, a secure feeling of readiness.

After six months of increased leg strengthening and aerobic dancing for stamina, I reserved a week at the ski school that had so impressed Steve, about ninety miles north of Montreal, Canada. Montreal wasn't cold enough in January. They had to put this school even further north into the tundra!

The classes were divided into forty groups according to descending ability, beginning at group 1. First, each skier was to come down a small hill. Waiting at the bottom were two instructors serving as judges. One of them would shout out a number as a skier passed by. That skier would then ascend the towrope to the main ski area and stand next to a flag that matched the number he was given.

Having arrived the day before classes began, I'd been taught briefly how to come down the small hill, referred to as the "bunny slope," and how to actually stop by creating a wedge or snowplow, a beginner's style of stopping downward motion. I was ready.

"Thirty-nine," he shouted to me.

A bit sullen, I took the towrope, ascended to the top, and found my group, "The Bad News Ski-Bears," group thirty-nine.

When everyone had arrived, the instructors bolted on the scene and shushed to a sudden stop in front of their respective groups, having pirouetted into a perfect "stem christie" (the advanced and graceful form of stopping, rather than the awkward and less reliable snowplow of the beginner). My instructor, Mike, proclaimed, "Okay, everyone turn and ski down that slope off to the right about fifty yards. When I stop and face you, all of you stop and face me as well." Fifty yards later, he stem-christied, turning to his left, and gracefully stopped while watching most of us snowplow beyond him further down the slope, some people having actually snowplowed into other people.

Gathering us together, facing him so that we were all perpendicular to the descending slope of the mountain, one leg slightly lower than the other to maintain balance, he said, "We will begin by working on turning and stopping." What happened next was a perfect illustration of how decisions that lead to balance and control—as well as gracefulness—can defy logic. It was a magnificent illustration of the futility of asking "Why?" as a prerequisite to making a decision.

"Okay, now everyone pay attention: Each of you, beginning with the person lowest in the line [who just happened to be me] will ski straight out about twenty feet across the slope; then, leaning into your downhill or left ski, so most of your weight is there, lift up slightly on your right, or uphill ski and turn." He demonstrated. Although it looked easy, I wasn't ruling out the possibility that it was a trick done with mirrors. I looked down the slope we had been standing on to the very bottom, where there was a road with cars going by, as well as trucks—big ones.

Then the logic began: "Why should I do that? I can't—that would be suicide. I mean, the mountain is already going that way, and he wants me to lean in that direction? Is he out of his mind? Maybe I should give him one of my business cards!"

I had a decision to make. Having taken high school physics, I recalled that a body in motion tends to stay that way—until it becomes roadkill! And in this case, my body could ultimately end up on a slab somewhere, which would have been considerably worse than Steve's casted leg. So the whole thing simply begged a "Why" question.

"Excuse me, Mike," I said. "Why do we lean into our downward ski when the mountain is already going that way? Are you sure about this? I mean, as just a beginner, why can't I just lean back a little so I don't end up . . . well, down there?" (A truck had just rolled by.) He simply said, "Because," and gave me a look as if to say, "I've been doing this for years—just do what you're told!"

Thoughts raced through my head: "Why should I trust him? Why can't I bring myself to lean into my downward ski as he suggested? Why am I having such difficulty deciding what to do?" I decided to opt for caution—so I thought—and to lean into my upward ski. This entire decision process happened in what seemed like a nanosecond.

I moved out about twenty feet, started my turn by leaning into my upward ski, and immediately fell, sliding down the mountain several feet. My skis had come off and both of my legs lay splayed out in opposite directions.

After being used as an example for the others, I was asked to do it again—correctly this time. So, gathering my skis, and myself, I tried it again, this time as suggested, leaning into my downward ski, even though logically it made no sense. In deciding to forego the "why," I let my body answer a better question: "How?" As in, "How is it possible that leaning in the direction of gravity will afford better control?" I actually defied gravity—or so it seemed—and turned gracefully (for a beginner), without falling and without barreling down the mountain out of control as I had feared when I couldn't decide to do it Mike's way.

Why couldn't I decide to trust Mike? A more useful question is this: What value did I get from asking "Why?" in relation to what seemed a violation of physics? His answer was to simply say "Because," implying that I should trust him (obviously not a very satisfying answer in view of the cars and trucks that were rumbling past on the road below me). My very next thought just before I leaned into my uphill ski was, "But why?" Once the question shifted to "How?", I did it as suggested, and obtained a useful result.

I also learned another very valuable lesson during that week of ski lessons. More on that later . . .

"WHY" QUESTIONS DON'T
LEAD TO GOOD ANSWERS

Inefficient "Why" questions can leave you feeling stuck, unable to decide. Why? Because, the "Because" that usually follows the "Why?" offers little comfort, insight, or opportunity to achieve the desired outcome: deciding. In effect, you get no good answers! Instead, you could end up flat on your bottom, wondering why what you thought made sense did not after all. To get back on your feet, try asking more useful questions. Here are a few examples:

1. "What specifically would result if I decided 'X'?"

2. "How would I know that deciding 'X' versus 'Y' is the better choice?"

3. "When (under what circumstances) is selecting 'X' more useful for me?"

4. Finally, "What else, if anything, would be affected by my selecting either 'X' or 'Y'?"

People become stuck when making decisions for a variety of reasons, asking inefficient questions such as "Why?" being just one of them. Let's move on to what it means to be *stuck,* and the various ways indecision and poor decisions manifest themselves.

CHAPTER 2

WHEN YOU'RE STUCK

Your life is the fruit of your own doing. You have no one to blame but yourself.

JOSEPH CAMPBELL

What does it mean not to be able to decide—to be *stuck?* Here we will explore various ways that getting stuck shows up in our lives, and some of the factors that contribute to not being able to decide, or deciding poorly.

It could be about a major purchase, or a minor one. Perhaps it's deciding what to order for dinner, what color paint to choose for a planned bedroom overhaul, or which bed. For some, it has to do with dating decisions, or what to do when there's trouble in the advanced stages of marriage—or in its very advanced stage known as "divorce." For others, it's about whether or not to ask for a raise, pursue a new career, or find a supplementary source of income in a second job.

And for still others, it has to do with a mode of chemical appeasement—cigarettes, alcohol, or drugs—following what they perceive to have been a difficult week. It could also take the form of succumbing to the seduction that sweets provide. For these folks, it eventually becomes a matter of whether or not to repair the damage that usually results to their bodies, and then, how specifically this can be accomplished. Some choices may include: joining a health club; jogging for free; enrolling in a self-improvement course; taking classes that improve body, mind, and spirit, such as yoga or Pilates; giving up smoking or drinking; or going on a crash diet.

Sound familiar? In all of these and other cases, what often occurs is that you come to the realization that a decision needs to be made, and one choice just doesn't seem to be any better than another. In short, you are stuck.

CHOOSING TO "NOT DECIDE" IS ALSO A CHOICE

Regardless of the context or the specific events about which they need to decide, for many people in our society, there are just too many choices. And sadly, this can translate into too many dilemmas. When it comes to having to decide, many of us just can't seem to get a foothold. Instead, our feet seem to be firmly planted in midair.

Can not. These two words reveal the true form of the contracted expression *can't,* and pose an interesting question: "What does *can't* really mean?" And, "How do we apply it in ways that prevent us from moving forward—from deciding?"

When people become stuck, they are at an impasse regarding a particular situation or event. As it affects your decision-making, *stuck* translates into becoming indecisive; you just can't decide.

When you stop and think about it, the phrase *can not* actually represents an ability, a talent that you have skillfully cultivated, often without fully realizing it. At some point in your personal history, in the presence of particular circumstances, you determined on the inside (in the form of thoughts or feelings) that you have the ability to *not decide* something. Therefore, along the lines of asking efficient questions, a more revealing and useful one than "Why can't I decide?" would be, "How have I become able to not decide?"

French philosopher Jean-Paul Sartre indicated that *not choosing* is, in itself, a choice. That particular choice can often instigate a series of personal events that keep us feeling stuck. For example, we can continue sifting the information—to choose something or not to choose it—back and forth. You know how it goes: "On one hand . . . on the other hand." This has been termed *dialectic thinking*, in which the consideration of one alternative suggests the presence of its opposite, which must also be considered. Using this type of reasoning to discover the truth goes back to ancient Greece, but for our purposes, can also lead to the choice of not choosing. There are other elements in the mix regarding how we become stuck . . .

WHAT IF I PICK THE WRONG CHOICE?

Deciding may be associated with a good deal of anxiety concerning the possibility of choosing the wrong thing. What if severe, negative consequences result from what I've chosen? How will I be perceived by others if I don't choose correctly—like an incompetent failure? Does the risk of recrimination for a bad choice outweigh the satisfaction that may be gleaned from selecting appropriately? Am I just acting like a victim by refraining from making a choice? *Why can't I decide?*

Although it's likely that learning to make confident, purposeful decisions is easier and less stressful than punishing ourselves for being inept, or remaining constantly at the mercy of outside forces, simply deciding cognitively to decide is often not enough to generate the finished product: a decision. After all, the cognitive part of us may also be screaming, "Yeah, but hell! What if I'm wrong?"

Still, within the cognitive realm, some people have success with what I refer to as *rationalizing reticence*—attempting to talk themselves out of being afraid of risk-taking.

"What am I worried about? There is no absolute certainty in life."

"We cannot guarantee that this favorable (or unfavorable) event will (or will not) occur."

"My deciding not to decide because I could make a mistake is as meaningless as deciding not to breathe because tomorrow the air-quality index may be poor."

"What's the worst thing that could happen if I do decide? You know, you really have to consider the 'worst-case' scenarios."

"I could die tomorrow. Then I'll really regret not having decided! Oh, wait . . . how would I know that? I'd be dead! Ugh! All this *thinking* about decisions is giving me a headache."

PICK *ANYTHING*—DO IT *NOW*!

Continuing along these lines, it is commonly believed that to overcome your hesitation, simply forcing the choice and making a decision, any decision—again, as a cognitively based activity (i.e., by rationalizing in one's head)—is a way of becoming *unstuck*. It is true that for many individuals who force a choice, there is an initial feeling of relief because they have gotten "off the fence" and taken some action. People who utilize this technique for deciding come up with some interesting methods: flipping a coin; selecting the choice that occurred to them first; or choosing the one that comes first alphabetically.

I sometimes find it humorous to watch people in a deli or similar establishment trying to decide what numbers to select when playing lotto, betting against the insurmountable odds that are inherent in this choice. At such times, I've found myself wondering how some of them chose to ask someone to marry them. Was it a random decision? Did they look at the worst-case scenario, imagining in living color how they would respond to rejection? Did they decide to pop the question as a way of simply getting off the fence?

Looking at worst-case scenarios as a way of talking yourself into the courage to become unstuck and decide something, in effect, involves betting against a risk. But it also illustrates a particular framework of operating—of behaving—and one that will be presented in one form or another throughout this book.

HOW WE ORGANIZE OUR CHOICES

We conduct our lives from within one of two frameworks: the *state of difficulty,* in which experiences are organized around problems and their avoidance; or the *state of what works,* in which choices are limitless, and therefore, an abundance of possibilities are available.

In her book, *Words That Change Minds,* Shelle Rose Charvet refers to several "motivational traits" that lead us to take actions of various forms. One such trait has to do with what it takes to get us moving. Charvet says that people are either motivated toward pleasure or away from pain. In the many contexts of our lives, each of us can possess some "toward" behaviors as well as some "away from" behaviors.

When someone who is stuck considers worst-case scenarios as a way of getting going, then his life in that moment is much more about avoiding an unpleasant situation or consequence than it is about achieving something of value. Under these circumstances, motivation is a function of moving away from pain.

How many of you would decide to wait until the last minute to study for a test when you were a kid? C'mon, 'fess up. When did you usually get your homework done, or do your chores around the house? When did the lawn get mowed? How many times did your mom or dad have to threaten to take away some privilege, or your allowance?

In contrast, how many times did your mom have to tell you to go inside and play a video game? Or to go and hang out with your friends? What about going to the mall, or a ball game? How long did it take to decide to do these things? Decisions such as these illustrate a different platform, a different motivational trait: moving toward pleasure.

These same motivational traits—toward pleasure and away from pain—carry over into adulthood. How many of you go to work for the fun of working, rather than to avoid being fired? You might say, "I go to work so I can get paid." But typically, there are those who view getting paid as a way of being able to pay bills on time and thereby *avoid* late fees or defaults of a more serious nature.

Let's paint with an even broader brushstroke to reveal the difference between these two motivational traits in adulthood: the criterion of job satisfaction.

How many of you are thrilled with your job? Do you consider your vocation your avocation—are you doing your "life's work"? Or rather, did you gravitate into the particular position you currently occupy as a way of satisfying parental urges for you to become successful? Do you work in your current field in order to avoid disappointing a significant other, such as a parent or a spouse/partner, and experiencing a sense of failure?

Or, in contrast, did you make a decision early on in your life to pursue a path that would not only be lucrative but also isomorphic with who you most understood yourself to be at the deepest level? In other words, when you considered this career path decision, did you experience a consistent comfort level through your body, thoughts, and feelings, which we refer to as a "match and fit"? Choosing your life's work as a function of it being a *match and fit* for you is clearly a "toward" behavioral choice.

Requiem for an Attorney

David, a successful attorney with a firm in New York City, came to see me to relieve his depression. He described a sinking feeling in his chest followed by a huge lump in his throat. Then he would run a lot of negative internal dialogue about how he was up against a brick wall with no way out, believing himself to be stuck and unable to decide the simplest of things. This explained why he frequently quarreled with his wife and avoided his children, lest he act short-tempered with them. They just didn't get it: He was so consumed with his pain that there was no time to address any of their concerns or issues.

Though he'd always had an ear for music, according to his parents, David was born to be a lawyer. David was very argumentative as a child, and yet so reasonable that his arguments were viewed as cogent. For years they joked, "You ought to be a lawyer!" And so, according to David, many of the significant people in his life encouraged him to become a lawyer, despite his real passion for music. He had even written several pieces of music for piano, which he was able to play. As he matured through adolescence and entered college, however, he seemed to be on autopilot in terms of deciding to become a lawyer. At first, he reluctantly learned to embrace it. This movement toward his chosen profession was reinforced by the fact that he excelled in his studies, and his childhood argumentative style seemed to serve him well in the mock-trial classes.

So he let the dust accumulate on the piano keys and he became a lawyer, eventually achieving success as a litigator. He married his childhood sweetheart and they had two children. They enjoyed life in their spacious home on Long Island's north shore. Making decisions as an attorney, of course, was easy for him; it was part of his success to choose wisely— everything from whether or not to take a particular case to adequately preparing his closing arguments. But as the years passed, an immeasurable sense of malaise came over him. So insidious was this melancholy that it was hardly noticed at first. Eventually he was consumed with the feelings that he labeled "depression," but he still refused to take medication because he feared it would cloud his judgment in court. He felt stuck when it came to deciding to leave the profession that didn't seem of his own choosing, and yet he was trapped by the need to subsidize the lifestyle he had cultivated.

At the root of it all was the fact that David longed for his music, an expression of his true self. I needed to help him "reset" to a posture of desire—a place from which he could conduct his life by being true to himself—without compromise.

Decisions to Serve Desire

What I did with David will become clearer in later chapters. For now, suffice it to say that when you decide from the posture of desire—a "toward" behavior—the possibilities become limitless. You are able to expand the landscape of your experience, a landscape that can become available to you as a resource in the future when, perhaps, another decision will need to be made.

When you decide to practice the piano in order to learn the various scales, or to develop finger dexterity across the keys to handle complex pieces of music requiring speed and accuracy, or to develop facility with transposing the key or the range of notes in which the piece was written, you are developing a set of skills by intentionality that may be used again elsewhere.

And so in high school, you can draw upon your music acumen when learning to type. The advantages of learning to type in this computer age are numerous, and lend themselves to acquiring even more skills in such areas as research, journalism, and communications, just to name a few. In the process, you certainly realize that you have expanded the "landscape," or the storable resources of the experiences you have accumulated, which can be used to acquire other skills.

By comparison, deciding to practice the piano so that your mom won't punish you by taking away your TV or computer privileges, for example, teaches you something else. Rather than placing a lot of attention and effort on the aforementioned skills, your piano playing is executed in service of avoiding a problem. And through time, what you develop facility in is just that: how to avoid problems.

Choosing to Avoid Pain

Let's look at another example in which someone made decisions designed to minimize pain, rather than maximizing pleasure and making selections that were a good fit for her.

A Life Filled with Emptiness

The purpose of living is to avoid dying. That is how Melanie conducted her life. Her decisions were all about preventing bad outcomes. She learned this from very strict parents who afforded her few opportunities to interact with people and to feel comfortable doing so, and they also consistently criticized her behavior. There were rules for everything—bedtime, studies, talking at the dinner table. In short, she made decisions based not on what she most embraced at the deepest level, but on what others told her was correct. In effect, she was living other people's lives from within her body. These were the seeds of her discontent.

As a divorced mother with one child, Melanie's restlessness flourished as she continued to manifest the values and behaviors instilled in her by her parents and teachers. Exhibiting a lack of social skills, she felt ridiculed by her peers, much as she had during childhood. Life was about choosing the least-painful alternatives and deciding to avoid what she didn't want to face and what wasn't working. She constantly complained about her job, avoided peers for fear they would ridicule her, and generally believed she lacked the ability to make useful decisions.

Melanie was constantly on her son, Byron, to do his chores, get off the computer, do his homework, turn off the TV, prepare his school clothes, set his alarm, brush his teeth, and get up in time for school—which he often did not—all for the same reason: to avoid the consequences of not doing so. Not surprisingly, like his mother, Byron made decisions that enabled him to avoid problems and punishment, and often had difficulty deciding what to do next for fear that it might be the wrong thing to do. Is that surprising? Socially, Melanie found as many reasons to move away from people as she found reasons to move away from the other activities in her life.

It became apparent that in order to help this individual, I would need to get her to change her method of decision-making. First, I uncovered her fascinations, preferences, and highly regarded achievements. Melanie has a penchant for computers. She speaks the language and can tame the most cantankerous box of bits and bytes. She programs, she cleans up "cybergarbage"—she can even remove viruses. Apparently, she passed this interest and skill set on to her son, who, by the time I stopped seeing Melanie, had begun writing code and was starting a kid-business: Web site design. Of significance, as you will discover later on in the book, when Melanie spoke about computers, her body shifted to an entirely different posture; she smiled, and her voice had a slight lilt to it. None of these qualities had been present earlier when she spoke about making decisions to avoid problems!

I observed a similar shift in her personality when we discussed some of her other fascinations, including comedy. The idea of this monotonic, depressive woman with an "away from" motivation strategy performing as a comedian was, in itself, comedic! Yet, this was a passion of hers.

The same could be said for her longtime interest in photography. Her pictures were crisp, colorful, and surprisingly detailed, and when she talked about them, she came alive in the manner described above. I spent the next several months guiding her into the position she held when she was consumed with these fascinations. By the end of our consultations, her language was replete with "toward" choices. She talked about deciding to start a photo Web site and how she would accomplish this; she was driven to complete a polished comedic product on CD that she would try to sell; and she began offering to troubleshoot problems with some of her coworkers' computers. Melanie had become consumed with what was "working" in her life, and she slowly began to shed the "away from" framework of deciding by which she had been operating.

This ultimately rubbed off on Byron: By the time Melanie and I parted, he had made the honor roll in high school; he had developed a small circle of friends; and he was continuing to develop his computer Web site business acumen. In the end, Melanie had decided to drain the emptiness from her life's container and fill it with joy instead.

The lens of a life being lived inside a state of difficulty is focused toward problems. Decisions that are made are usually in service of avoiding those problems—often, worst-case scenarios. Clearly, Melanie had gone to great lengths to avoid those events and activities she deemed as potentially dangerous or anxiety-provoking, a way of being that was fed to her through the input of significant others from early on in her life.

STUCK—THE CHOICE TO NOT DECIDE

When a problem cannot be avoided easily, indecision—also known as simply *being stuck*—happens. When you are stuck, your attention, having been focused on avoiding something, likely failed to move you away from any alternative that would have constituted a real decision.

Eve, the Universal Donor

A thirty-eight-year-old nurse—let's call her "Eve"—had been married for a decade to a man she had met in the hospital and whose health she had helped to restore. Patrick had cirrhosis of the liver, caused by years of alcohol abuse that he often flatly denied. His liver was not the only part of his life that had become cirrhotic: He had lost two jobs in three years; he had an ex-wife from a previous marriage; he'd lost countless sums of money. The circumstances of his life were largely related to his addictive behaviors that involved making *away from* decisions, those that momentarily minimized pain. He'd even lost his freedom, as he had been incarcerated for disorderliness and DWI.

Eve had gotten to know Patrick when she'd cared for him during his two-month hospitalization. She had felt sorry for him, thinking that the misfortunes that had befallen him had resulted from circumstances beyond his control. Believing Pat to be a good person, she dated and then married him, all within a one-year period following his release from the hospital. He had been hired as a warehouse foreman shortly after being released from the hospital, and he'd maintained a steady work schedule—until he and Eve had been married for three months. The altercation that cost Patrick his job, in his mind, was not his fault, any more than the fact that, having been fired, he had felt the need to drink, stay out all night, and, when finally arriving home, engage in an argument with Eve that ended in violence—violence that led to his being removed from the house with an order of protection in place for Eve.

During the next few months, Eve developed some symptoms of stress, including sleep disturbance, stomach upset, difficulty concentrating, and difficulty making a decision about anything—but especially, whether or not to end her marriage. Although her husband had had little difficulty deciding to drink again, and then to become violent with Eve, she was, after all, a caregiver. She didn't want to appear callous and insensitive; she equated ending a bad marriage with abandonment, and so, she became stuck.

Eve made a decision to *not* make a decision, and, as a result, was paralyzed by the situation in which she found herself. For Eve, getting stuck this way represented her fear of the consequences that could result from whatever decision she made, as well as her confusion about the next set of choices that would be before her if she made the decision to leave her husband—choices having to do with finances, safety, and her ability to choose men wisely, for example.

Sometimes when you are stuck, if a particular decision is crucial to attaining something you desire, choosing to not decide will affect that outcome adversely as well. Suppose on your way to work one morning, your car (with 125,000 miles on it) finally comes to its final resting place: the middle of the highway. You call your boss and explain the dilemma, and you take the day off in search of a new family car. Having seen a few different brands and models, suddenly you find yourself unable to decide between two criteria: gas mileage versus durability/safety. On the one hand, there is this cute compact that will almost get you from here to Germany on a single tank of gas; on the other hand, it also seems like you could lift this little car right up onto the sidewalk, should parking ever become a challenge.

In contrast, there is another model that struck you as a suit of armor on wheels, but failed in the gas mileage department. Stuck regarding your choice, and fearing that making a decision will result in an error in judgment (or certainly something less than perfection), you choose to not decide . . . which could definitely impact your goal of obtaining a raise at work in a negative fashion.

The *Myths* That Govern Decisions

Mike Krzyzewski, the revered men's basketball coach of the Duke University Blue Devils, once said, "The truth is that many people set rules to keep from making decisions." Eve's rule was that you don't abandon your husband because of his limitations; that makes you insensitive. Those rules that prevent decisions are part of the *myths* people live by that inhibit them, myths such as, "Life is a compromise that requires sacrifice," or "A good person always turns the other cheek." The concept of myth and its relationship to decision-making will be further elucidated with examples in chapter 10.

There are those who believe, as Eve did, that their only choice where decisions are concerned is to become *stuck*. All attention is organized around moving away from deciding anything, except not deciding. Then there are those such as Melanie who were able to get going, but only in service of moving away from unpleasantness, still not living a life based on deciding what she wanted. In effect, this is a specific kind of "stuck," in that you are still not deciding to move forward based on what you want to be in your life, as your future pulls you toward those outcomes. Instead, you are moving forward by being pushed from behind, as your decisions are governed by a fearful past.

Becoming unstuck often involves making big decisions. Big decisions require big risks, which requires courage. Facing those risks directly and accepting responsibility for the act of deciding—including when those decisions render unexpected outcomes—is difficult. As you proceed through the various stages of your journey here, you will encounter cases in which individuals decided, *exquisitely*. That is, their decisions were a *match and fit* for who they truly were at the deepest level, evidenced from a particular position held within the body, rather than having their decisions reflect the input of others disseminated through time.

In truth, what facilitates facing risks, accepting responsibility, and making an exquisite decision is more than meets the eye. It involves more than words can describe—the words you tell yourself and others in the course of asking, "Why can't I decide?", and then trying to become unstuck. What facilitates facing risks in the course of deciding exquisitely also involves more than trying to sort through conflicting thoughts. Rather, this facilitation actually begins within your body, as you will soon discover.

Facing the risks, which facilitates making good decisions, also has to do with where you place your attention when it comes time to decide things, and it's time to take a look at that now.

CHAPTER 3

IS THIS YOU?

It's easy to make good decisions when there are no bad options.

ROBERT HALF

Most people who become stuck when it comes to making decisions have some things in common:

1. They begin by placing their attention on all of the aspects of a situation that they do not want to be present—the problems and the negatives—which does not help them discover what they actually do want.

2. Then they try to corral all the negatives by looking at things like worst-case scenarios as a way of getting off the fence and deciding.

3. If they do arrive at a decision, at best it will be one of managing pain rather than seeking pleasure.

Is this you?

In contrast, what would life be like, decision-wise, if you could begin to place your attention where you want it, thereby making a decision based on the glass being half full rather than half empty?

SO MANY CHOICES

Sometimes getting stuck and becoming indecisive happens when we generate a flurry of choices that seem to overwhelm us—choices that come at us faster than we are able to process them. When this occurs, we can sometimes feel overwhelmed, so we start to shut down, fearing that we might make the wrong decisions. Then we become stuck in the mire of indecision.

Majoring in Uncertainty

Lottie left college after her sophomore year. That was the first of a series of decisions she made as a budding adult. Three more important decisions followed: She married the man she had met one summer while still in school; she remained married for seventeen years, raising their three children through adolescence; and then she divorced her husband.

After having made these decisions, Lottie decided to make one that would affect only her life: She decided to return to school and finish her degree. Elated when she discovered that the school of her choice would accept on transfer the credits she had previously earned at her first college, Lottie enrolled for the fall semester. That choice was easy.

More difficult was the choice she now faced: "What am I going to do there? What should I major in?" She just couldn't decide. It had been a no-brainer to decide to get married and have children. And when she discovered that her husband had been unfaithful—for nine of the seventeen years of their marriage—deciding to divorce him had also seemed logical. But when it came time to decide something in relation to her own pursuits, she was filled with uncertainty. Lottie decided that for now she would not decide. She opted for the common "no-pref" major, which is to say that for now, she would be majoring in . . . not knowing what to major in.

An Unfit Outfit

The saleswoman offered Gina a price that she never could have imagined. She knew the outfit fit her well. And you know what they say: "If the outfit fits, wear it" (well, you get the general idea). But the only thing that seemed to be wearing at that moment was Gina's patience. Ever happen to you?

You just can't seem to decide, despite the fact that a particular something apparently looks sensational on you. Even when three people tell you how great you look in the outfit as you stand primping in front of the store mirror, you just can't decide what to do. Then the fidgeting starts. "Hmm . . . yeah . . . no, wait. Oh, I don't know; maybe I shouldn't." Then come the doubts about where you would wear it: too formal for this, too casual for that. Despite evidence to the contrary, it just seems easier to simply not decide—at least, for now. Sullen, confused, you just let the decision slip through your fingers. And you leave the store.

The Trip to Exhaustion

"I want to take my wife on vacation. We've both worked very hard this year and we truly need to get away for a while. I know she likes water—the blue-green water of the Caribbean delights her. I like that, too. Bermuda is lovely, very romantic. But it's pricy. But then, how much is her happiness worth? What if it rains? There's no gambling. Maybe we should go someplace that has gambling in case it rains. Aruba has gambling. But wait, that can get expensive. What if we get carried away playing Texas Hold 'Em and spend too much? What if we start losing and think, 'Maybe if we stay here a little longer, we'll recoup some money,' and then lose some more? No, gambling isn't the answer. Or is it? Atlantic City is closer. So is Mohegan Sun—no airfare. She can feel the exhilaration of being there with the shows, too. But wait, what about the beach? Oh, I'm exhausted! Maybe we should just stay home with a nice bottle of wine, get in the hot tub, and rent a movie."

The Blunt Ax

"Senior management from the Seattle home office sent word today that we have to dismiss 314 people from their jobs: a handful of first-line supervisors, some sci-tech folks, and a whole bunch of support personnel. As third among middle-management directors, I've been given the responsibility of sending 250 of them packing. The plant director will handle the remaining folks. I get that we need to curtail personnel costs while increasing productivity, a somewhat paradoxical task. I just can't decide on the criteria to use as a basis for firing what amounts to 15 percent of our workforce. Should I go with relative work output—or lack thereof—over a comparative period of time? How about poor attitude and incompatibility with fellow workers? Incident history? Cost-effectiveness in terms of number of raises received in the past year? Or should I use some other criterion entirely? When it comes to establishing the grounds for what I have to decide, I feel like my feet are firmly planted in midair!"

An Indecisive Palate

"*Je ne sais pas encore*," the young woman responded to her server, appearing a bit overwhelmed and offering up her indecision in decisively good French. "*Il y a tant de choix délicieux.*"

"*Pas de soucis, Mademoiselle, rien ne presse,*" the server replied, now turning to her date, who looked like a fish out of French water. "For you, *monsieur?* Have you decided?" asked the server, taking on a blasé tone.

"Hmm . . . I'll just have what she's having."

"*Monsieur, 'Je ne sais pas encore',* means, 'I don't know yet.'"

IN THE BEGINNING, DECISIONS ARE EASY

One of the most difficult of life's activities for many people is making a decision. But for a certain special class of people, decisions seem to come easily. At any given moment you may hear them expressing exactly what they want, or nixing what they do not. They are known as *children*.

How many children do you suppose have difficulty deciding to watch TV, play a video game, or text-message someone? Do you think they worry about what could go wrong if they do? Can you imagine a child thinking, "I'd like to watch *The Ghost Whisperer,* my favorite TV show, but what if this week's episode isn't good?" Often children—like animals—make many mini decisions throughout the course of a day without hesitation—decisions about oral gratification, play, satisfying their curiosity, and achievement of a particular outcome.

As children grow into adolescence, then adulthood, they actually learn how to become indecisive! This happens as a result of some interesting factors that occur, as you will soon learn.

DRINKING FROM THE HALF-EMPTY GLASS

Ultimately, as we mature, the perspective we acquire in making decisions is that of the half-empty glass; most of our decisions are based on what is *not* working in our lives, and these are poor decisions. We attend to what we identify as "issues" or "problems," to which we respond with feelings of stress, uncertainty, depression, and confusion, among other negative choices.

Too often adults learn to become choice-phobic. And the only thing they know for certain is that they are not sure. Sometimes it's simply uncertainty about such topics as what car to buy or whether to go out for dinner at an Italian or an Indian restaurant, and then, what to order. Of even greater significance is the uncertainty that may arise in relation to deciding whether or not to seek new employment, or, having done so, whether or not to accept an offered position. And in the case of Eve from the last chapter, sometimes being indecisive carries pernicious consequences, such as being stuck in a bad marriage.

We make hundreds of decisions each day—big ones, small ones—and many occur outside of our awareness. How many of you actually plan to touch your nose each time it itches? Or scratch your head? Or even place one foot in front of the other as you navigate your way to where you are going?

Yet most of our decisions are made in relation to what is not working in our lives. They are "away from" decisions—those that help us avoid problems, or at least, try to do so. They are, in effect, poor-quality decisions. That is because decisions that merely serve avoidance behaviors do not move us "toward" a particularly defined goal. They fail to lead to new information or expose us to new situations of which we may become conscious and act upon with intentionality. In short, they do not expand the landscape of our experience.

As a batter facing different types of pitchers, you learn how to time your swing according to what is being thrown your way. Given the many small decisions that comprise swinging a bat, you may eventually learn how to place the ball in the direction of your choice, as well as to drive it a long way if that is your desire. You learn that such decisions are directly related to the type of pitch you are facing—fastball, curveball, change of pace, knuckleball, and so forth. Each type of pitch requires that you make subtle shifts in your positioning at the plate as well as your swing of the bat. These "shifts" are decisions of intentionality. The landscape of your experience as a batter becomes broadened.

In contrast, if you choose not to face certain pitchers or are designated by your team manager as a "designated bench player," a sub who by comparison faces fewer pitchers, you may feel more threatened at the plate. Your expectations about being successful and either getting a hit or working a walk will be compromised, and this will affect decisions such as whether or not to swing or where to stand in the batter's box. In short, the landscape of your experience—your ability to make useful decisions that will become resources, which can be used to foster future decisions—will be very narrow.

When we feel stuck and make poor decisions, concentrating on what is not working instead of what is working, our attention is centered on what we identify as issues or problems. And the responses we make as part of those decisions are too often accompanied by feelings of stress, uncertainty, depression, and confusion.

Look at the following reality checklist and answer either yes or no to each question.

1. Do you feel like you are chained to the problems in your life?

2. Do you support that feeling by watching the nightly news, replete with stories of death, destruction, and financial woes?

3. How about gossip shows that reveal astonishing minutiae about famous people, so you can share stories the next day at work around the watercooler?

4. When you awaken, do you run that "little voice" through your mind, announcing what you can expect to go wrong today?

5. Are you often aware of a knot in your stomach at decision times?

6. And after all that, do you try not to notice what isn't working—to no avail?

If you answered "no" to all of these, you can skip the rest of this chapter and move on. For the remainder of you who answered "yes" to even one of the above, keep reading.

HOW TO LAND ON YOUR FEET

Have you ever heard the myth that a cat always lands on its feet? This is primarily true due to the cat's vestibular system (sense of balance), but often is expressed as a metaphor for having a quick mind and a sense of where to place your attention. If you want to "land on your feet," you need to place your attention there, not on what could happen if you don't, or on what other part of your physiology might experience the landing instead. To begin making better decisions, you need to drink from a different glass, one that's filled to the brim. Try these:

1. Train your brain to begin "noticing for" (perceiving) what is there rather than what is not there. Close your eyes and become extremely still. Breathe deeply through your abdomen and expel the air.

2. Now open your eyes and pay attention to what you see and hear around you. Get a firm handle on what you feel on the outside, as opposed to your internal feelings. That is, pay attention to the position of your body. Feel your feet warming the bottom of your shoes; sense the secure embrace of gravity holding you to the earth, and the earth to you.

3. Go about your business—walk, drive, shop—and in these moments, continue to notice through your senses (sight, sound, feeling) what is around you. Consider the world around you and all it contains.

4. Finally, for now, begin to place your attention on something you would like to be "true" for you. For example, "I am going out to buy seafood for tonight's dinner"; "This afternoon, I am taking the time I need to exercise at the gym"; "When my husband comes home, I am definitely broaching the topic of this year's vacation."

5. You need to retrain your brain to become facile in a different kind of noticing for—a way of paying attention that detects what is possible rather than what may or may not be a problem. In effect, becoming unstuck and making useful decisions is a choice you make primarily by noticing for anything else in life other than what leads you to become stuck.

Skiing by Design

After we had finally learned how to turn on skis, Mike set us loose to practice. On one run down the mountain, a new set of decisions presented itself to us. Bordering the slope on each side was a thicket of trees, so dense that you could get lost there . . . forever. Sort of like "the rough" in golf, only instead of losing a ball you could lose yourself!

Moving left to right, I noticed, peripherally, that I was getting closer to the rough. And just as I began my turn by leaning into the downward ski, as I had learned the hard way that morning, I slipped, fell, and slid toward the "Black Forest"! Gathering my skis, reattaching, and continuing, I skied in the other direction. That rough on my left seemed very far away, because my "lie" was now way to the right. But in skiing transversely right to left, I noticed that those trees to my left were closing in on me fast. Once again I fell and stopped short of hitting a tree on that side. This happened several more times until I reached the bottom. I had become apprehensive, and was putting all my attention on that damned forest!

Every decision I made involved moving away from one of those trees. After all, like the signs (which didn't help) stated, THE WOODS ARE AS DARK NOW AS THEY WERE 200 YEARS AGO. ALWAYS SKI WITH A BUDDY. I could be lost forever, like a golf ball!

I decided to raise this point with Mike. It turned out that most of the group had the same concerns. Mike seemed pleased that I had given him an easy segue into his next lesson.

"Randy wants to know how to avoid the trees on the perimeter of the slope. Anyone else have that concern?" Everyone acknowledged this. "It can be real dangerous, you know. Anybody read the signs posted along the way on all these trails?" Several people recited the message in unison, about how little the forest had changed over the past 200 years. "You have to be really careful not to slide into the trees, understand?" We all began shifting our weight, nervously. "When you ski, be sure to have a buddy with you, just in case." More nervous shifting. Everyone in the group now saw the glass as half empty, for sure!

"Of course, there's another thing you can do to avoid ever hitting those trees." He paused; time seemed to stop. The group held its collective breath. Then he proceeded to show us how he traversed the slope without hitting any trees. We watched him zigzag down about fifty feet, and then sidestep back to us.

"What did I do differently?" he asked. He had actually done something highly significant: He had made a series of decisions that had nothing whatsoever to do with avoiding the trees. They were "toward" decisions—those designed to achieve something that was intended.

Mike continued: "In order to not hit the trees, you need to ski as if they are not there." *Easy for him to say,* we were thinking. "From a standing stop, as you are now, think of the slope as a geometric form—think of a triangle's leg, for example— and plot your path to the end of that form. Begin by drawing an imaginary line from where you are now to a point on a slight downward angle out there. At that point, you will initiate your turn, leaning into your downward ski. Immediately, you will draw another imaginary line across the slope to the next point, ski there, turn, and do it again, and so forth, until you reach the bottom. Any questions?"

It worked! When I got to the bottom of the ski slope, I thought about Mr. Mortimer, my tenth-grade geometry teacher. I wondered if he had ever skied, and if so, whether he had decided not to think about the Black Forest.

Learning to ski was about making a lot of decisions. There were basically two choices: decide by identifying and then trying to avoid problems; or decide by placing attention where it was desired most and achieving the intended outcome.

What became clear in relation to making life's decisions is stated most eloquently by Dr. Joseph Riggio, architect and designer of the Mythogenic Self Process, a set of powerful tools for learning to live life true to yourself without compromise: *Where you place your attention is where you will get your result.*

A useful corollary to the above aphorism is: *Always place your attention where you want it most.* Perhaps it is becoming a little clearer why people often can't decide. They place their attention where they want it least—on problems—and as a result, become stuck and either choose to not decide, or make poor decisions in relation to the avoidance of something unpleasant.

As a beginning skier, my attention was definitely on avoiding getting hurt, or killed. I was very aware of that densely populated forest that guarded a dark secret, one that had existed in that form for over 200 years, according to that sign! And the more I considered all of this as I skied down the slope, the closer I came to all that I feared becoming a reality.

In contrast, when, as Mike suggested, I skied as if the trees "were not there," my attention was elsewhere: It was on turning, effortlessly and with poise and grace. (Well, again, as much as could be expected from someone who only moments earlier had envisioned himself as either roadkill or lost in the wild.) But then, I chose to stop thinking about all that stuff, and I never ended up with tire marks on my face or lost in those 200-year-old woods!

In a similar way, for years, clients have approached me with requests to help them in ways that typically began with deciding to rid themselves of some unwanted event or experience. "Can you help me get rid of my anxiety?" "I need to get over my depression."

"I can't get my son to stop daydreaming and do his homework." "My husband won't communicate with me. The more I try to get him to come out of his shell, the more he seems to withdraw." "I get nervous when I have to speak in front of a group at work." And the list goes on . . .

As you have discovered from the ski story, placing attention where you do not want it fails to allow you to decide in favor of what you truly do want. Often, when we place attention where we want it least—becoming stuck and either deciding not to decide, or making a poor choice—this can have another, more harmful effect, and one that can adversely impact our health.

Making decisions and your health will be examined next.

CHAPTER 4

HEALTHY AND
UNHEALTHY CHOICES

It is easier to prevent bad habits than to break them.
BENJAMIN FRANKLIN

So far, it has been suggested that people either make useful decisions by considering an array of possibilities and desires, or by choosing those that will lead to avoiding negative consequences. And when believing they are neither able to move toward desires or avoid negative consequences, what results is the decision to not decide, a way of being stuck.

In every case, at the biochemical level, a decision will either have a self-enhancing effect on our health, leading to a positive outcome and resulting in an almost-simultaneous release of positive neurochemicals (like endorphins), or a self-injurious effect, leading to the release of stress hormones (and others) that are debilitating to one's health.

At the behavioral level, poor decisions—or, at times, the failure to act, otherwise known as indecision—can lead one to engage in behaviors that may carry unpleasant consequences, and that at times can be injurious or life-threatening as well.

Here, we will examine the reciprocal relationship between addictions, bad habits, emotional distress, insufficient exercise, and matters of judgment, and the resulting poor decisions that can be made.

POOR DECISIONS THAT "TOAST" YOUR HEALTH

When people smoke, experiment with drugs, or binge-drink for the first time—whether because they are looking for socially acceptable ways of fitting in, or because they have just reached the legal age limit and want to celebrate—they are making conscious decisions that are not in their best interest.

Sometimes, others become conflicted and decide they can't decide whether or not to join the crowd. They are simply stuck in the world of indecision, which often negatively impacts their health with stress indicators such as headaches, muscle tension, sleep disturbance, gastrointestinal distress, emotional withdrawal—even depression (i.e., negative self-statements, crying, and suicidal gestures such as cutting).

For teens and young adults who are still dependent upon their parents, either because they are still in school or otherwise living at home, the contexts in which decisions occur include friendships, love interests, family tensions, and the pressures associated with academic performance at school. More often than not, people within these social strata still make decisions using what is referred to as an *external frame of reference.* That is, they look to others for feedback as to how they are doing, and they are motivated to choose by moving away from pain. So they will seek to avoid peers in whose company they feel threatened, and begin drinking, smoking, using drugs, or overeating as ways of combating tension. In all cases, these choices have an adverse effect on their health. Of significance is the fact that this pattern of deciding by moving away from pain, adding in whatever substances will cause that to happen, often continues on into adulthood and old age. In short, you will find that many of their parents are like this, too.

The unhealthy choices people make set off a destructive cycle of events. First, the perception of pressure in the various aspects of their lives, such as home, school, or work, with colleagues or peer groups, often leads them to make the very same poor choices mentioned above. Then these choices "feed" or increase the tension they experience, which in turn leads to more bad choices, and a recursive loop is formed.

CHILDREN LEARN WHAT THEY LIVE

The poor decisions teens make often mystify their parents. When the younger set is faced with having to decide, given fewer perceived choices, they may withdraw and become stuck, or make choices based on worst-case scenarios. Bewildered parents have approached me, unable to understand what in their teen's life could be that stressful. Furthermore, these parents themselves are feeling stuck, and have related time and again that the choices their kids are making don't seem to make any sense to them. They are certainly not the choices they (the parents) would make under the same circumstances.

And yet, these same parents were once teenagers who often decided to "toast" their own health through excessive alcohol consumption, cigarette smoking, drug usage—often cocaine and marijuana—and overeating. Many have come to my office reeking of cigarette smoke, sometimes of alcohol, and often overweight or undernourished, with reddened, irritated nasal passages. Some describe how they choose fast food over health-conscious meals due to time constraints, and then complain that their son or daughter makes unhealthy decisions. In reality, they have inadvertently modeled the very choices they decry in their children. I refer you to Dr. Dorothy Law Nolte's famous poem, "Children Learn What they Live," written in 1972, attesting to parents as models of what in effect are good and bad decisions.

Adult clients often tell me that their lives, with their attendant stressors, justify the making of unhealthy choices in order to survive. Surprisingly, they are baffled by what their children describe as the stressors in their lives. I've often asked certain adult clients if they thought it was a contest—that only when someone has *really* experienced stress should he be allowed to make poor choices that compromise health. This comment usually serves three purposes: (1) It makes parents more sensitive to the needs of their children; (2) It makes parents more sensitive to the futility of their own poor choices; and (3) It models better decision-making for their children.

NOT-SO-GREAT EXPECTATIONS

Poor decisions can take several forms and compromise health in many ways. At times, poor decisions are a way of putting off better ones for fear of failure; other times, they just arise from sheer laziness or carelessness. And then a catalyst can come along and change all that . . .

Exercising Options

Lenny B., a thirty-eight-year-old single chiropractor, sought assistance with making decisions. He described himself as having a poor self-image, believing that this contributed to the quandaries in which he often found himself. Lenny was frequently stuck, as the decisions he made were not in his best interests.

He seemed concerned about fitness and his health, especially because he wanted to impress Teresa, a woman whose picture he had seen online and whom he was to meet for the first time that Saturday. She was a professed athlete and Pilates instructor.

Since they were both avid golfers, Lenny decided to ask Teresa to join him for a first-date round of golf, followed by cocktails. Wanting to make an outstanding first impression and thinking that Teresa would not be as attracted to his lanky, skin-and-bones appearance as she would be to muscle, he decided to join a gym and work out at a feverish pace before his date, which was a week away.

At the gym, he encountered a muscle-bound hulk sitting on a bench curling a dumbbell. Lenny approached him, saying, "Excuse me . . . hi. I'm new here."

"Hi. I'm Charlie," was the response.

Lenny continued, "I've got to tell you that those are the biggest biceps I think I've ever seen. They're actually bigger than my legs!"

Charlie laughed.

"Charlie, do you mind if I ask you something?"

"Sure—what's up?" Charlie put his dumbbell down and looked at Lenny.

"You know, I'm wondering, do you think I could ever get a set of biceps like yours?"

"Sure, Lenny," Charlie said, reassuring him. "What you

need to do is come here to the gym, three times a week for four years, and do the series of exercises that I will write down for you, and then—"

"Three times a week?" Lenny interrupted. "For four years? No, wait, you don't understand. I mean . . . I have this really amazing date—a knockout, and very athletic. She has no idea what I look like. I told her I stay in shape. I can't wait four years. I need to have those muscles by this Saturday!"

Charlie looked at him incredulously and said, "Len, I get that you are in a rush to have results soon, but let me ask you something: If you come to the gym and follow my exercise routine for the next four years as I suggested, how old will you be then?"

Lenny thought for a minute, and replied, "Forty-two. But—"

Charlie interrupted. "Right. And if you *don't* come to the gym and do the exercises, how old will you be in four years?"

Lenny, appearing confused, muttered quietly, "Forty-two— and still skinny." The lightbulb went on—he'd gotten it.

You see, he was going to get older regardless, but his ability to make a useful decision was affected by an unrealistic, immediate desire to impress his date, which was now compounded by the stress of anticipating being out with her and displaying a body that could make her laugh and ultimately reject him. He was trying to make a good decision for a poor reason—clearly an "away from" motivation strategy.

The day after that encounter with Charlie, knowing that he would be meeting a woman without the benefit of Charlie-like muscles, Lenny wanted help building different muscles:

the kind that exude emotional self-confidence. He wanted to be *present* for Teresa, and also to be accepted for who he was, yet he also had the sense that he had been making unhealthy choices by not exercising, and he wanted to commit to building his body, slowly, over time.

I told him a brief story, the essence of which is this: Muscleheads often use the expression "no pain, no gain." But Lenny was at a crossroad where there were two kinds of pain: the pain of discipline and the pain of regret. The first involves embodying the learning required to make a useful decision that positively affects your health and leads to becoming successful. The other one is simply making excuses for not having done so, the likely choice of someone who expects failure and therefore chooses to move away from pain. In effect, he could decide to either spend time doing the work required to achieve what he wanted, or lament the fact that he did not.

Then I had him close his eyes, breathe deeply from his abdomen, and locate a place within himself where he felt his system come to rest—where it was most balanced and centered. Upon opening his eyes, I had him imagine deciding to commit to the exercise regimen that would improve both his physique and his health. In the process, I had him cite several advantages that would emerge from this decision, such as increased bone density and flexibility, better muscle tone, resistance to disease, and more self-confidence.

Once he'd decided to commit, I had him shift his body into the position he believed he would hold when he achieved the body Charlie had told him about—*in four years.* This included his posture, breathing, and way of speaking, and how he would feel when he looked in the mirror. Then, holding this "future memory" posture, I had him decide to share these revelations with Teresa as a reflection of his genuineness and motivation "toward" (rather than "away from") a particular choice—a healthy choice.

ALCOHOL, SUBSTANCE ABUSE, AND JUDGMENT

Making decisions that relate to using *good judgment*—that is, evaluating the alternatives and making a choice that is safe, self-enhancing, and most likely to produce the desired outcome—also has a direct impact on the health of those involved. Too often, people—both young and old—take risks when driving under hazardous conditions such as in fog, rain, snow, or ice, or while under the influence of alcohol and other controlled substances.

Making a decision to consume or abuse alcohol or drugs can have a deadly effect on your health. Moreover, it can also create a negative situation with regard to the decisions that lead to and result from those substances.

Say you're out with some friends celebrating an occasion, or simply the fact that it's Friday, the day when you decide that after a stressful week, the best way to get rid of that stress is to toast the weekend. But sometimes in toasting the weekend, you may become *toast*—as in what happens when you burn your health! So after tipping back a few and feeling tipsy, you may decide you've had enough, and that it's time to leave. On the way home, the alcohol in your bloodstream impacts some other decisions: where to turn and when; whether to run that yellow light; how fast to drive;

or how much braking distance is required to avoiding hitting the pedestrian who is crossing the street ahead.

The decisions people make while driving under the influence of alcohol lead to specific consequences—serious accidents that could involve a fatality, DWIs (police citations for driving while impaired, which means manifesting a blood alcohol level that exceeds the legal safe driving limit), disorientation, and property damage, to name a few. In other words, the decision to drink or use drugs can lead to specific health consequences, which will then impact any decision you make following the alcohol or drug consumption—and the cycle continues.

Approximately 14 million people in the United States are chronic alcohol abusers, or are considered addicted to alcohol. Another 4 million or so use any of a variety of drugs for recreational (not medicinal) purposes on a regular basis. Every time someone ingests alcohol or uses a drug, he is making a decision, and a poor one at that; 40 to 50 percent of all incarcerated inmates who committed violent crimes chose to drink or use drugs. The National Highway Traffic Safety Administration estimated that there were at least 17,000 traffic fatalities related to alcohol and drug use during the past three years, and alcohol is the third leading cause of preventable deaths in the United States.

The consistent and excessive use of drugs and alcohol inevitably leads to poor choices that often kill other people, whether in accidents or as a result of violent crimes. And these poor choices often kill the abuser too, as alcohol causes a number of physiological changes in the body, including killing brain cells and inducing erosive gastritis, which can limit the absorption of nutrients and vitamins and lead to brain damage, memory loss, loss of sexual responsiveness, sleep disturbances, and psychosis, as well as Wernicke's encephalopathy and

Korsakoff syndrome. Then there are those alcohol- and drug-related decisions that break up marriages, cost jobs, alienate children, and at the physiological level again, adversely affect the health of newborn children (fetal alcohol syndrome).

Are drinking and drug use actual choices or decisions people make, or are they diseases? *Alcoholism, alcohol dependence,* and *alcohol addiction* are terms that imply the choice of whether or not to drink is taken out of the person's hands—or mouth. These terms reflect the position that alcoholism is a serious if not fatal disease for which there is treatment—one that sometimes includes drugs, but mostly involves counseling and twelve-step programs, such as Alcoholics Anonymous (AA). The latter model is based on several assumptions, including the fact that the alcoholic is helpless and cannot do it alone, and that there is help out there, which requires surrendering yourself to a higher power.

The twelve-step programs imply that those afflicted are incapable of making good decisions and therefore need input from others outside of themselves to make better decisions. This model has extended into other realms in which making decisions can lead to negative consequences. And so now, in addition to Alcoholics Anonymous and Narcotics Anonymous, there are organizations like Overeaters Anonymous, Gamblers Anonymous, and anger management workshops, to name a few. All of these share the assumption that there is some underlying disease process that seriously impedes your ability to make useful decisions.

Many believe that since the American Medical Association (AMA) proclaimed alcoholism a "disease," it is beyond reproach. However, the disastrous results of these choices notwithstanding, there are many who believe that behaviors such as excessive alcohol consumption, smoking, or overeating are not diseases, per se.

Irrespective of your position on this issue, remember that making poor choices directly leads to other bad decisions, and believing they are within your domain to change can lead to making self-enhancing decisions to improve your health. An example is the aforementioned case of driving after drinking. To the extent that excessive drug and alcohol usage remains a choice, its opposite also exists as a choice, and so does an opportunity to change for the better.

THE INFLUENCE OF ANXIETY AND DEPRESSION ON DECISIONS

So why would someone decide to use these substances if the risk is so severe? Often, the decision that is made in relation to alcohol and drugs is an "away from" decision—an attempt to appease an emotional state such as anxiety or depression. Depression, like alcoholism, is often considered a disease. However, whereas there are observable negative changes in the brains of chronic alcohol users, often accompanied by deterioration of their vital life signs, there is little if any research to support the contention that depression is a disease. Yet, almost 19 million American adults are affected by some form of depression, which includes a variation labeled *bipolar disorder*.

Perhaps a more surprising statistic is that the collection of symptoms and behaviors comprising anxiety disorders affects nearly 40 million adult Americans and is considered the most common mental illness in the United States. People with an anxiety disorder are three to five times more likely to go to the doctor, and six times more likely to be hospitalized for psychiatric disorders than those who do not suffer from anxiety disorders.

As you will discover in later chapters, often times people who are diagnosed with depression or an anxiety disorder have made poor decisions by placing consistent attention on the problems in their lives. These decisions are then held within their bodies in a compromised posture that also adversely affects their health. Such decisions frequently cause the release of neurochemicals that represent the body's response to stress: There is a constriction of the blood vessels, increased heart rate, reduction in oxygen efficiency due to a withdrawal response within the chest cavity that restricts lung capacity, and many other deleterious physical events.

Experiencing these and other related emotional states (such as panic disorder), individuals will often compound the negative decision-making process by deciding to try and make life better with alcohol and drug usage. The immediate effects of these substances divert attention from those emotional states. In effect, alcohol and drugs can lead someone away from *noticing for* problems in the short term.

But what if someone could learn to notice for what is *possible*—a "toward" motivation process—using tools other than chemical additives? Is it possible to shift the ground you are holding—the position of your body, what you notice for, tell yourself inside—so not only will you make decisions that move you away from substances, but also toward something else; something that is the antithesis of anxiety and depression?

A SLIM CHANCE IN THE WAR ON FAT

"I've dieted successfully—hundreds of times!" Is that you? If so, what it means is that, given the opportunity to select from among a variety of foods, you made some healthy-choice decisions for a while, but then resorted to deciding to choose less-than-healthy foods.

As with alcohol consumption and drug abuse, overeating decisions are often in service of placating other limitations, such as anxiety and depression. When someone either decides he or she *can* not decide, or decides poorly to embrace worrisome thoughts and feelings associated with anxiety, it is not uncommon to believe that there is nothing out there to feel good about; thus, *feeling good* is accomplished by deciding to eat sweets and other unhealthy foods, which, in abundance, compromise health and, in many instances, perpetuate the very emotional states one seeks to eliminate through food! For example, once you have finished eating a distracting snack, the event that prompted your anxiety is still there—only now it's accompanied by the guilt of unhealthy overeating. Additionally, tempting foods that are often consumed to quell negative emotional states are often high in sugar and high on the glycemic index. This means they cause huge fluctuations in glucose and insulin levels, spilling those substances into your bloodstream and causing a definite health hazard.

Whether you decide to overeat or to go on a diet, both decisions can be poor ones, and may lead to a failed outcome: losing weight. As a result, life becomes either feast or famine. Perhaps feeling sad or anxious, you choose to overeat. Then, feeling guilty, you decide to go on a crash diet, convincing yourself that this will quickly eliminate those unwanted pounds and relieve the guilt for having accumulated them. As a result, you become caught in that cycle of repeated weight gain and weight loss, never able to lose body fat. In fact, this unsuccessful dieting regimen at times can actually increase body fat!

When you eat foods that are high on the glycemic index, those foods are digested quickly and turned into body fat very easily. The reason for this involves your body's historical genetic makeup. A long time ago, before the advent of the health club, cholesterol, and dieting, there was widespread famine. People did not live long enough to die from obesity-related diseases (and you think you have problems?). Everything was fast food—all you could eat—and contained huge quantities of animal fat and carbohydrates high on that glycemic index. A bulging belly was testament to one's ability to store energy, ready to be called into action during times of danger or famine. Those with a gut that could store fat survived longer. Hence, this biochemical quality was "selected" through generations, which means your body became really skilled at storing fat.

Today, attempts at maintaining long-term deprivation diets meet with failure due to the availability of forbidden foods, and successful advertising. Despite your best intentions to eat healthy veggies and avoid lots of carbs, we too often fall victim to temptation and take a bite from that forbidden fruitcake or mound of pasta. Suddenly, your body will induce "famine mode." In effect, anticipating lean times ahead, it tucks that piece of cake away in your belly bank account as if it were the last day on earth.

Then you decide that this is no good, and what you need to do next is go on a very low-calorie crash diet. This creates an unfortunate paradox: When cutting calories, your metabolism reacts to this would-be starvation problem by slowing down. A slower metabolism burns less fat. As a result, you accomplish the opposite of the intended effect, minimizing your weight loss. To make matters worse, having taken this measure, you are now likely to be very hungry. So you decide to eat higher-calorie foods once again. But watch this! Your body, meanwhile, still reacting to the threat of famine induced by the crash diet, will begin storing it as fat again. The result is that too often, deciding to diet with a low-calorie regime, followed by a return to higher-calorie foods, may actually *increase* your body fat and reduce lean muscle mass!

Now, before this becomes all too overwhelming and you decide to not decide and become stuck, there are better choices afoot. One involves those very feet—aerobic exercise, of any kind: walking, running, jogging, or swimming, to name a few. Another healthy choice is deciding to redistribute the calories you already consume throughout the day by changing *how* you eat.

Here are a few suggestions:

1. Decide to eat dinner early, as the body is more efficient at storing fat after six o'clock at night.

2. Eating smaller portions more frequently helps, too. The production of insulin in the body facilitates fat storage. Eating smaller quantities more often stabilizes insulin at lower levels in the bloodstream, reducing the likelihood of storing fat.

3. Decide to go grocery shopping only after you have consumed a meal.

4. Eat slowly and chew your food thoroughly. This serves both to reduce the intake required to feel full as well as promoting healthier digestion.

5. Keep reading to learn how to access a highly positive posture within your body, associated with good decisions,

and in which you notice what is possible. That way, you will be emotionally healthier and will be less likely to use food to placate bad feelings.

BUTT OUT

Smoking—like overeating and, at times, alcohol and substance abuse—is an excellent example of deciding in the moment, and deciding poorly. Choosing to smoke often follows other poor decisions, such as the decision to feel and act depressed or anxious.

Those who smoke decide to do so in spite of compelling evidence that it will eventually kill you. The Centers for Disease Control (CDC) report that deaths from cigarette smoking exceed 440,000 per year. The CDC further estimates that smoking trims twelve years off an average life span.

Yet, when people feel stuck or otherwise make poor decisions in other contexts, they often decide to utilize a poisonous substance to feel better about their other bad choices in life. As in the case of alcohol, people who smoke heavily often believe their poor decision is really not a choice—that their bodies have already made that choice for them, and they call it an addiction. And yet, millions of people have chosen to make the healthy choice to quit. There are many methods for accomplishing this. Here is Dr. Green's prescription:

1. Purchase only one pack of cigarettes at a time. This choice will adversely impact your finances since they're more expensive by the pack than the carton, and this may begin to protect your health.

2. You have to decide you really want to quit in order to achieve the next step. So if you are a smoker in the precarious position described above, put this book down for a minute and ask yourself if you are truly ready to live longer. Take your time . . .

3. Welcome back! Here's the next step: Remove every cigarette from the pack. Obtain a very fine-point gel pen. Write the name of one of your children on each cigarette. There is no hard-and-fast rule for this; let's not get dramatic and make this still one more major decision. If you have three children, divide the cigarette and name distribution accordingly. Put them back in the pack. Do this for each and every pack you buy when you first buy it.

4. On the outside front of the pack, using a magic marker, write in large letters, PLEASE DON'T DIE, MOMMY (or DADDY).

5. The positive posture referred to in step 5 above in relation to overeating, more thoroughly described later in the book, can also be applied to smoking cessation.

TO SLEEP, PERCHANCE TO DREAM

Thousands of individuals suffer from an extreme form of sleep deprivation known as insomnia. Frustrated, exhausted, and frightened, they just can't seem to *decide* to sleep. Unique to this sort of limitation is the paradox, "Be spontaneous!" You can't decide to do something that happens involuntarily. Let's try something. I want you to decide to blink. Some of you may begin to notice more rapid blinking or the opposite—your eyes are tearing up as you valiantly fight the urge to do something that happens outside of your awareness. Now let's look at a similar example, where something about which you are usually unaware becomes unavoidable: Try to not feel your left ear. Ladies, don't pay attention to your left earring, *right now!* What happened?

Poor decisions related to sleep manifest as futile attempts to induce this spontaneous event on purpose: *trying* to fall asleep— hence, the "Be spontaneous!" paradox. You might decide to utilize everything available to you, consciously—pills, warm milk, reading, alcohol, and exercise—in order to achieve that precious sleep. And, as in so many other instances of unhealthy decision-making, you do it again and again. Under the circumstances, it is not uncommon for an insomniac to believe he's tried everything and that nothing works.

One of the more consistent features of insomniacs is that they deliberately pay attention to those experiences that cause them discomfort. Some examples include: lying in bed picturing what they are going to do when they confront their boss, spouse, or friend, or running a little voice in their heads that worries for them.

Of course, worrying through negative internal dialogue is, in and of itself, an unhealthy decision, and often provides the opportunity of avoiding certain unpleasant tasks. When sleep is not happening, ironically, it becomes one more thing to worry about, thereby preventing its occurrence! In attempting to try and sleep, some people make the inadvertent choice to stay awake. Perhaps it's time to make a healthier choice—something different for a change:

1. *Try to not sleep.* Instead of spending countless hours tossing and turning, and busying yourself with activities designed to make something spontaneous (sleep) happen on purpose, resolve yourself to the decision that you will not sleep tonight—that it's totally unnecessary and that you cannot allow it. Read a book or watch TV—but never in bed.

2. *Count sheep, not problems!* If you must stay awake nights, at least turn off the "internal dialogue from hell" that keeps you pondering your problems through your darkest hours. Instead, experience a pleasant fantasy, in living color. For added effect, tune into the sounds that fantasy would include, and pay attention to the feelings that may develop. For example, imagine yourself lying on a beach on a clear, warm, sunny day. Notice the bright colors of the water and the contrasting sand, the various shapes around you. As the crest of a wave curls inward, crashing against the crushed pebbly shore, you can hear that sound and feel the spray of mist on your face, its salty taste on your lips. Enjoy the warm feeling from just having lain in the sun.

3. *Get tired.* During the daytime, be sure to engage in at least an hour's worth of aerobic exercise; and finally . . .

4. *Learn to access the positive body posture* related to living life from what is possible rather than *noticing for* problems. Inherent in that posture is the idea of "letting go," an essential ingredient to allowing the spontaneous activity of sleep to capture you!

EXCEEDING LIMITS AND UNHEALTHY CHOICES

There are other types of "judgmental" decisions that can seriously impact your health, particularly those where you mistakenly believe you have either the skills or necessary information with which to make a good decision when, in reality, you do not. The results can not only be embarrassing at times, but may also pose a serious health hazard.

An Engineer's Train of Thought

Engineers are an interesting group. While nothing is absolute, don't tell them that! They expect that, given their train of thought derived from applied mathematics and logic, they should be able to solve any problem. And so, in addition to applying this logic to their jobs—such as an IBM engineer would do—they frequently believe that they can also take apart an ailing boiler, or fix a washing machine, a television set, or a dishwasher.

Not long ago, a client reported to me that the heat in her home was not working. Members of her family were bundled up in heavy clothing and blankets and nestled by the fireplace while Dad, the IBM engineer, was downstairs trying to fix the furnace! After a week of futility and dismay, he finally relented, and his local oil company sent a tech to the home.

By this time, according to the engineer, there were apparently two parts left over that he couldn't find a place for, anywhere! The oil company tech just laughed. The family was cold, having been without circulating heat for over seven days. Even the fireplace was unusable because the engineer/

father hadn't cleaned the fireplace flue—for five years—and of course, had refused to allow a chimney sweep to do so.

Additionally, unbeknownst to the engineer or his family, the furnace was old and contained a few tiny cracks, which increased the risk of toxic fumes being emitted into their home, an obvious health hazard.

Despite his best efforts to fix the furnace, Dad the engineer finally recanted his poor decisions and deferred to the judgment of his oil company repairman. He opted for a healthy choice: a new oil burner, which was installed in less time than it would have taken to try and fix the old one, with its two leftover parts.

DECISIONS THAT STOKE THE SLOW BURN OF STRESS

Less obvious a health risk than deciding to use drugs, drinking, smoking, overeating, or overestimating the skills necessary to secure an outcome is making a choice that leads to stress that builds slowly over time—stress that increases heart rate, blood pressure, stomach distress, sleep disturbance, and more. Such choices include situations in which a student—adult or child—skips class, or when homework fails to be completed or turned in, frustrating a parent who incurs further negative consequences from her child's teacher.

Then there is the stress that arises from either making poor decisions or deciding not to decide in situations that involve social interactions. An example might be, "I want to ask Judy and Bill and Margie and Frank over for dinner, but my husband doesn't like all that company. What if he says no?" Or, "I want my boss to notice the outstanding work I've accomplished this quarter. I want him to see me remaining at the office after hours! But I don't want to do anything too obvious that makes him think I am simply seeking his approval rather than doing the work because of my personal dedication. I can't decide how best to make my statement."

Marital conflicts, finances and financial planning, ferrying children to their various activities and school-related events, major purchases, and work are among still other typical areas in which decision-making can affect health. Each decision may typically be associated with stress responses that can include breathing changes, muscle tension, sleep and eating disturbances, and gastrointestinal distress, which will then have an adverse effect on the decisions that follow. Stress and decision-making will be further examined in chapter 7.

NLP AND UNHEALTHY CHOICES: THE "INSIDE" SCOOP

Dr. Richard Bandler believes we make thousands of unhealthy choices every day. He is the codeveloper of Neuro-Linguistic Programming (NLP), a model that describes how people create internal sensory experiences, such as pictures, sounds, and feelings, that lead to a particular set of behaviors, and how they can modify this perception and thinking on the inside to create more useful behaviors on the outside.

Bandler's position is clear: What you think and feel is connected to what you do. When you feel bad, you will make bad decisions. Hence, being in a bad mood is not conducive to making good decisions. So, in the case of alcohol abuse, when someone is running a lot of negative internal dialogue about what will go wrong today—or already did—or when life's vicissitudes seem to force his hand, the decisions he makes will not be self-enhancing, but rather self-injurious.

THE EMBODIMENT OF GOOD DECISION-MAKING

Along these same lines, the NLP model states that what you do on the "inside"—how you hold your expectations of success or failure—has a direct impact on the decisions that result. This is a major premise of this book in relation to becoming unstuck and making useful decisions.

What you do on the inside, beyond thinking or feeling bad, has to do with the *position* you first hold within your body a nanosecond before those thoughts and feelings occur. These positions we hold are fundamental to the decisions we make, and that's true literally as well as cognitively or emotionally. In fact, in order for you to have a thought or feeling, that experience must first manifest as a physical position within the neuromusculature of your body. This initial position you hold for each and every experience is known as the *somatic form,* and is comprised of micromuscular flexions, postural shifts, breathing changes, and eye-accessing cues (the way your eyes move to locate and retrieve information).

The somatic form you hold at any given moment mirrors the way you perceive your environment. That is, your somatic form represents whether you live your life based on possibilities or problems. As you know, where you place your attention is where you will get your result, and people who place their attention where they most want it hold a particular positive somatic form in relation to making useful decisions; those who place attention exactly where they don't want it—on their problems—hold themselves in an inhibitory fashion that often leads to indecision and poor decision-making.

Decisions bear a reciprocal relationship to your health: They can both affect your health and be affected by it. This, in turn, often leads to making additional poor decisions, which further compromises your health, and so on.

Several types of situations in which you may experience either being stuck or making decisions that are self-defeating or unhealthy have been introduced. So how do you suppose this all happens? How did you get this way, anyway? I'll bet you think it has something to do with events that occurred in your past. Lots of people would agree with you. Let's take a look at a few of those avenues through which indecision and poor decision-making may have developed.

PART TWO
HOW DID WE GET THIS WAY?

CHAPTER 5

LOOKING BACK TO
MOVE FORWARD

*The worst pain a man can suffer: to have insight
into much and power over nothing.*

HERODOTUS

So far, we have discussed some of the typical ways people tend to get stuck: how they end up deciding to not decide, or how under certain conditions a decision will be rendered that is not in someone's best interests.

In this chapter, you will be introduced to the idea that past events in your life may inhibit present decision-making, as illustrated by two prominent theories of human development. When we allow the events of our past to inform the present, such as explaining why we can't decide something, we are said to be bringing *insight* to bear on the situation. Let's take a look at how insight-oriented approaches attempt to explain both indecision and decisions that are poorly conceived.

When someone asks why he or she *can* not, there is often a temporal consideration implicit in that "Why" question: "When did this first happen to me?"

THE PAST INFORMS THE PRESENT

Throughout the past century, there have been a number of theories and models designed to show how past events and experiences can inhibit desirable behaviors in the present. These theories and models attempt to explain why we get stuck in the present, why we become indecisive or select poor choices. Things that occurred a long time ago—either events to which we fell victim, or specific activities of which we were a part—damaged us in such a way that we became incapable of performing in some fashion. Two of the most prominent models, with examples, are examined below.

FREUD'S PSYCHOSEXUAL THEORY AND DECISIONS

The psychosexual theory of development created by Dr. Sigmund Freud, and those whose theories emerged shortly thereafter, known as "neo-Freudians," represent how past so-called "damage" hampers our present performance, including making decisions.

Freud's theory is based upon what he referred to as "psychodynamic principles," which collectively serve as a metaphor for explaining our everyday functioning. By illustration, we are structured in such a way that left unchecked, the part of us that is pure impulsive emotion, the *id*, a vast reservoir of evil, unconscious erotic and aggressive energies, would run amok, seeking immediate discharge into the environment. Think caged animal for a moment. These impulses are controlled by another structure, called the *ego*. Its main job is to help an individual navigate the course of his everyday life by controlling those unwanted id impulses that occur as he interacts with his environment. The ego is sort of the zookeeper of your mind. It spends time tending to the id's impulses, feeding it, containing it, giving it time to express itself, and putting it "to bed."

Much of the ego's energy is devoted to controlling those unconscious id impulses (by using a series of what Freud referred to as "defense mechanisms"), while a certain portion of that ego is devoted to conscious daily activities. Decisions are considered to be unconsciously motivated, as the ego is pressed into action in service of protecting the individual.

Highly relevant to the ability to make useful decisions is the development of *insight.* Simply stated, insight occurs when unconscious impulses and other stored phenomena become conscious.

As someone develops insight, there is also less need to defend against those volatile id impulses. Moving in this direction, the ego can divert some of its energy associated with id work to more-conscious activities, such as making decisions. In effect, then, to the extent that insight is minimal or even absent, the ego is kept busy trying to keep the lid on the id—those unwanted, evil, sexually based impulses—and less ego energy is available for the functions of conscious awareness, including making decisions. The result: Those who lack insight are often indecisive.

In Search of a True Art Form

Marty, a senior at the Cleveland Institute of Art, was facing graduation. In recent months, however, both due to the paucity of jobs in the art world and his confusion regarding what he wished to pursue as his life's work, he had become ambivalent about pursuing a career within the field of art. This had caused him considerable anxiety—loss of appetite, trouble sleeping, gastrointestinal distress, and occasional headaches. Lately he had been running a lot of negative internal dialogue over his dilemma. Though he once believed majoring in art would eventually lead to a decision about his life's work, completing this course of study had left him confused, disillusioned, and longing for the days when he could just party on the weekends and generally live in the moment. He loved being around other people and believed that, as an artist, he would be spending a lot of time alone.

His parents' expectations were also complicating matters regarding his career choice. Early on in Marty's life, his paintings had inspired his parents, a guidance counselor, and his parents' friends to make flippant remarks, such as, "You could be the next Monet," and "You really should study art, or maybe architecture."

Comments like these, alluding to what he "should" be when he grew up, had led Marty down his current path, and to his dilemma. What was he to do after college? In this confused state, people often go into the wrong professions (for them), which make them less useful to themselves and society.

In psychoanalytic terms, the power to be decisive is the responsibility of the ego (the reality part), which has the role of controlling the excess id (libidinal, sexual) energy. It does this by generating what Freud called "defense mechanisms." One such defense mechanism, sublimation, represents the morphing of sexual energy into something more socially acceptable—a decision that is more useful for an intended purpose.

Sublimation would have accounted for Marty's selection of a major and his subsequent enrollment in art courses—a movement toward his seemingly inevitable vocation. There is a channeling of the ego, leading to enhancement of the skills gleaned from class work, as well as proficiency in his overall artistic ability, due to the fact that the energy of the body and mind has been directed toward one course of life (work). What is inherent, according to the psychoanalytic principles in this example, is that the young man must use his ego to consciously direct all forces and the energy of self-gratification to the acquisition of skills as it relates to vocational choice, and then to the vocational choice itself. In order to reverse the irrationality of man, he must deliberately and consciously choose what will continue his existence and survival over those volatile id impulses that serve to merely gratify him at the most primitive level.

So, Marty's career choice or decision is dependent on his ego's ability to control the irrational impulses of his id. Conversely, the roots of his indecision lay in the failure of his ego to curtail his sexual (id) energy.

As Marty became increasingly disenchanted and confused regarding the prospect of graduating from college and actually engaging in the field for which he had prepared the past four years—to begin generating a return on his parents' investment in him, both financially and emotionally—more of that id energy began bubbling up than could be contained by his ego, and he became consciously aware that he could neither decide to go with what his parents thought best for him nor what in his gut seemed right for him. He was stuck—indecisive. (Think Dustin Hoffman in *The Graduate*.) And this extended into his counseling with me.

After an initial two visits to discuss what had brought him in, he decided that he just couldn't decide, and that no amount of counseling was going to change that. His essential dilemma: He couldn't choose between what was inculcated in his mind (the external information from his parents about what should be true for him) and what he somehow knew within him was true (what Freudians would attribute to uncontrolled id energy).

He was given another set of choices: to leave counseling and continue to experience the characteristic unrest of indecisiveness, or remain in counseling and come to understand how he could learn to trust himself—his own body and mind—as a compass that would lead him in the direction of useful decisions. He chose counseling, which in itself represented the first in a series of good decisions, those that were most consistent with what he knew at the deepest level was the right thing for him to be doing.

Just prior to graduating, the lightbulb went on in his head, as he described it: He applied for and eventually accepted a position on a team of creative artists at a major advertising firm, where he could be around a lot of people and express his "id energy" in creative and socially acceptable ways.

Again, decisions are made as a function of man's ability to reverse the irrationality that is forever fomenting just beneath the surface of his conscious awareness. Deciding effectively depends on your ego's ability to control the would-be destructive impulses that emanate from deep in your unconscious while working to consciously develop insight into where your skills truly lie, and how your existence can best be sustained.

CARL ROGERS: HOW DECISIONS ARE INFLUENCED BY OTHERS

Another theorist, Carl Rogers, saw people in a much more positive light than did Freud. Essentially, he believed people were capable of living fulfilling lives (which he called a state of "self-actualization") when they developed a healthy self-concept. This would occur to the extent that their primary motivating force in life (which Rogers called the "organismic valuing process") remained untainted by artificial "conditions of worth" that develop during the acculturation process from childhood to adulthood.

As part of the approval/disapproval process of significant others, particularly parents, we are taught to adopt their value system. To be deemed worthy as a son or daughter, you are taught, through time, to think and feel in a certain prescribed manner. This sort of relationship is further fostered by adult models within the school system, as well as by society at large—everything from how to behave in a restaurant, in relatives' and friends' homes, on public transportation, or in the library, to situations in which there are legal ramifications, such as whether to use a potential parking space, whether to obey a traffic signal, or how to behave in a courtroom. This process can extend to decisions about education and future endeavors, and even who to choose for a mate. In short, through the process of acculturation, we can become disconnected from our internal awareness (alignment) of who we most know ourselves to be, as a function of those "conditions of worth" that are accrued from others.

According to the model set forth by Rogers, the feedback we receive from others—often in the form of disapproval or requests to change in some way—tends to diminish us as people by compromising our self-concept. Furthermore, because those with a poor self-concept often assimilate the values of others as if they were their own—either from others' requests to change or as a result of disapproval—those values are actually "artificial," according to Rogers. A poor self-concept coupled with artificial values certainly impedes the ability to make a good decision. When someone is forced or influenced to adopt values divergent from his own, his "organismic valuing process" (i.e., his perceptions—what he knows to be true for him at the deepest level within his body), which is the source of naturally good decision-making, becomes diverted from its goal of self-actualization. This leads to either poor decisions, or, at other times, the decision to not decide. That indecisiveness or poor decision-making occurs in service of pleasing others, or to comply with a faulty, unfavorable self-image—definitely not decisions that are to one's own best advantage. Let's look at a case history from the Rogerian perspective.

The Lady with the Lamp

Sally B., a single, twenty-seven-year-old woman, is a bartender in a busy restaurant. In recent weeks, she's become withdrawn for no apparent reason, and unable to work. Of late, the simplest decisions—what to wear to work, what to eat for breakfast, even what movie to watch—have become overwhelming. Requesting some time off, she's retreated to her apartment to begin reflecting on her life.

Sally knew she wanted to become a nurse as early as the age of six. Her inspiration, almost from the time she first learned to read, was Florence Nightingale. A child prodigy, Sally was reading historical novels by the age of seven.

By the time she was ten, Sally had spent many evenings talking to her mother about the interesting achievements of people she deemed remarkable, especially Florence Nightingale, nicknamed "the lady with the lamp" because she was tireless in her pursuit of aiding others. Of particular interest to Sally was Florence Nightingale's diligence and dedication as a "sick nurse," and her contributions that led to reforms in nursing care. Sally saw her as an inspiration, and an excellent model of perseverance and accomplishment.

When Sally regaled her mom with tales of her reading adventures, Mrs. B. was very often "elsewhere." She barely made eye contact with Sally, often interrupted her curtly, and at times made derogatory remarks about her aspirations to become a nurse. To her mother's way of thinking, there were other more important issues in life.

One evening while Sally was relating a tale of Nightingale in the Crimean, her mother chimed in: "You know, Sally, ya gotta be careful who you trust in this world—lots of folks out there have their own fish to fry; they ain't gonna take care of you. Most people don't give a damn, dear; it's the cold hard truth. They're just out for themselves. If you don't take care of yourself, no one else is gonna!"

Sally was stunned by this conversation, as she had been many times before, when, seemingly for no apparent reason, her mother's train of thought had drifted away from Sally's point to one that was laced with overly cautious admonishments. Mrs. B., a hardworking divorced woman who possessed little formal education, meant well and was very protective of her children—especially her daughter.

Mrs. B. needed to take a second job when Sally was twelve years old, which meant that Sally often had to cook and clean for herself. She spent many hours alone after school, as her mother forbade her to have friends in the house when she was not home to supervise. After all, you can't trust strangers.

Stressed, tired, and growing ever more cranky, Mrs. B. became less tolerant of Sally, and began criticizing her for the smallest of things—a room less than tidy, dishes in the sink, homework not completed, and ultimately, a violation of one of her rules: no kids in the house.

Sally missed her friends, but she also felt sorry for her mom, whom she realized had made some difficult choices in life. She didn't want to end up like her mother, yet she began to notice that she was having difficulty making decisions when her own best interests were at heart. More and more, she would decide in favor of what her mom would have done under those particular circumstances. Her reading time diminished—after all, there was so much to do around the house, and if she didn't do it, her mom, who was holding down two jobs, would have to. Not only would that make her mother angry, Sally thought, but it would be unfair to her.

As Sally progressed through her teens, she became more efficient in completing both schoolwork and housework. But she had progressively withdrawn from her peers, citing a lack of time for socializing. The presence of other girls made her uncomfortable. She had neither the funds nor the desire to keep up with them and their pursuits—movies, shopping, boys.

Sometime in her mid-teens, having long since abandoned the idea of nursing school, Sally became aware of something else: She couldn't make a decision. She wasn't sure about a lot of things, especially whether or not what she had done would please her mom. Feeling extremely guilty and emotionally drained, she would say to herself, "What's wrong with me? When did all this start? Why can't I decide?"

Years later, having passed up two opportunities to marry, Sally entered counseling in an attempt to find what she had lost: her self, as in her "self-esteem." What she learned during the next seven months changed her life for the better. First of all, based on the Rogerian paradigm, Sally learned that she had accumulated "conditions of worth," meaning that the frame of reference she used to make decisions was totally external. Over time, she had cultivated the limitation of needing others' approval in order to make a decision in any given situation.

Second, she needed to "find Sally," beginning by paying attention to the things that mattered most to her. Though she had long ago abandoned the idea of becoming a nurse, Sally had never lost her passion for Florence Nightingale and her courageous achievements as a nurse and health reformer. She remained highly motivated to make a difference in the lives of others. Recognizing that she was still an avid reader and someone who wanted to make a difference in the lives of others, her counselor suggested that she begin reading about innovative social reforms and interesting medical advances.

Finally, although her past had exerted such a monumental influence on nearly every decision she'd made up to this point, she was taught how to let go of the past and become mindful of the present, with an eye on the future. She was still "the lady with the lamp," in her own right, but now her light shone in a new direction. Three years later, she was well on her way toward graduating college with a political science degree. Sally had decided that she wanted to help people by shaping the system through her work as a state congresswoman.

THE EFFECT OF INSIGHT ON CHOICES

Psychoanalytic, Rogerian, and other insight-oriented theoretical approaches share a common feature in the quest to understand how we became unable to decide or learned to decide poorly. These approaches involve traveling back in time and reliving difficult aspects of our lives that led to issues we now confront—perhaps an inability to control irrational impulses, or the adoption of values not our own—to uncover deep, hidden, inner meaning behind the reasons why we make poor decisions, or none at all.

In the next two chapters, we will examine how trauma and stress—especially in early childhood—can impact our decision-making skills, and particularly how events in the past may cause indecision. As you may recall, this is referred to as *developing insight.*

We look back in an attempt to uncover deep, hidden, inner meaning behind poor decision-making because insight produces change. If you can just figure out how you got to this point, and ultimately went wrong (i.e., develop insight in the form of hindsight), you can fix it. This makes a lot of sense to a variety of theorists and helping professionals. It appears reasonable that if you can simply understand what is blocking you from deciding or otherwise causing you to make poor decisions, you will suddenly feel unburdened and able to start making useful choices.

Insight Exercise

1. Think of something—a purchase, a subject, perhaps an interpersonal matter—about which you frequently have difficulty making decisions.

2. Then, consider a challenging time or event early in your life that could have caused your current indecisiveness— perhaps an irrational impulse that led you astray or otherwise caused some difficulties in your childhood, or a recollection of frequent instances of disapproval from a significant family member. Take all the time you need to consider each and every instance in which you currently either can't decide or decide poorly.

3. Once you have gained insight into these matters, consider to what extent you can now make decisions that are free of conflict. In other words, ask yourself, "Did gaining knowledge from my past about a possible reason for my current difficulty enable me to move beyond it and decide?"

Then, let's move on . . .

CHAPTER 6

THE AFTERSHOCK OF TRAUMA

All children have to be deceived if they are to grow up without trauma.

KAZUO ISHIGURO

Here, we will explore the influence of traumas both early and later in life—those events that produced panic, persistent worry, and other recurrent unpleasant emotional states—and how they relate to decision-making problems. We will also examine the relationship of trauma to rigid thinking, in which alternatives are black or white, as well as how all of this is held within the body.

Some theorists believe our very beginnings are traumatic in the sense of separation from the mother. This idea has been stated in numerous places, most notably by Otto Rank, in *The Trauma of Birth*. One manifestation of this trauma is that from our safe, warm, soothing, nurturing beginnings, we are suddenly cast out into the cold, noisy, fast-paced, and strange reality called the world. Following birth, trauma may occur in a variety of ways during childhood. Sometimes, it will be events that are unexpected, like a bad fall or accident that results in a life-changing injury; other times, they are unthinkable situations that shock us to the core of our being, such as sexual or physical abuse, family rejection, abandonment or neglect, or withdrawal of support, solace, and affection for reasons that are mystifying to a child.

TRAUMA AS A ROOT OF INDECISION

In an article entitled "The Client's Wounds: Trauma and Decision Making," attorney Rick Kammen and Dr. Lee Norton consider trauma to be present when someone experiences "events that are outside the normal range of daily experience and highly threatening to our physical and emotional well-being."

Moreover, when these types of situations occur, and an individual believes his or her safety is at risk, uncertainty sets in as to what choices to make in order to resolve the situation. As a result, there is a perceived loss of control.

According to Kammen and Norton, when traumatic events are present, a person will often become stuck and unable to make a decision for fear he might choose badly. The uncertainty that is often perceived by someone in a traumatic situation can also generate highly negative physical states as well, such as agitation, gastrointestinal distress, sleep disturbance, worry (manifested as a steady stream of negative internal dialogue, for example), and headaches, to name a few.

At times, these authors note, "a fear of judgment by others is a contributing factor to the reluctance a trauma victim often feels when having to make a decision."

So, for those who have experienced some form of trauma, the essential process of decision-making can be experienced as traumatic in itself. When you feel challenged, perplexed, and anxious, what often results is indecision.

THE INFLUENCE OF ARISTOTLE: *THIS-OR-THAT* THINKING

Dr. Norton and many other researchers, therapists, and professionals within the fields of psychiatry and psychology share the view that

those individuals who have experienced trauma are primitive think-
ers for whom things are *this or that,* or *either/or*—not both. Furthermore, the fact that they have become this way is attributed to some
irreversible developmental process of which trauma is an essential
part, collectively referred to as "damage."

Someone who has experienced childhood trauma, or has had
that experience compounded with additional trauma later on as
an adult, is seen as having been damaged at various junctures in
life in ways that are basically irreversible. This includes the apparent polarization—you against me, *this or that*—which is often
expressed by those who feel pressured to decide while also believing they are trapped within a situation that ostensibly prevents a
decision from happening. At best, according to many in the field,
we can help people modulate their response to future challenges as
the need to decide occurs.

The process of this-or-that thinking has been referred to as
Aristotelian logic, and refers to a process of choosing that was
founded on the "law of the excluded middle" (everything must be
classifiable as one thing *or* another) and the "law of contradiction"
(a thing cannot be *both* one thing and another). Thus, Aristotelian logic, the kind we are most at home with and which seems
intuitively obvious, stipulates that something cannot both be itself
and not be itself at the same time. Hence, this or that; you cannot
choose both.

As you will discover as we proceed in subsequent chapters,
people are taught to organize their lives in terms of this-or-that
equivalents: You can either go out and play *or* learn in school, for
example, but not both. When it comes time to decide something,
there is no frame within which the concept of "this *and* that" can

exist, because it doesn't serve the society that operates from the functional framework of this *or* that.

There is no compelling reason, for example, to force the members of our educational system—from the upper echelons of bureaucracy down to the classroom teacher—to be both playful *and* educational. Why is it better to teach kids in a classroom, organized into rows facing the teacher, than it would be to take them out into a field on a beautiful spring or autumn day and teach them there? Well, in accordance with the functional framework organized by our society, it has been reasoned that when these children graduate, they will need to be trained to operate indoors, in offices and businesses that resemble the schools in which they were educated.

The classroom provides such a situation: an orderly, enclosed environment that does not allow individuals to make instinctive or intuitive decisions for themselves; an environment in which they need to follow the rules without exception or question, and to obey authority, even if they have internal experiences (within their bodies) at the deepest level, telling them that a particular choice is not a *match and fit* for who they know themselves to truly be and, therefore, not the right thing to be doing. This is done with the knowledge that a preferred decision is being sacrificed in order to gain the approval of those members of society—parents, teachers, employers—who control access to what is perceived as desirable.

So we are conditioned to have to choose from distinct alternatives—*this or that*—when it's time to make a decision. And those who have experienced trauma and find decision-making itself to be almost as traumatic in a sense, will frequently opt to decide *not* to decide, or may, under duress, force the choice and choose badly.

ATTEMPTS TO HEAL TRAUMA
BY SELF-MEDICATING

It is not surprising that among those who report having experienced some form of trauma in life, many turn to self-medicating as a way to feel better, choosing alcohol, drugs, overeating, gambling, and so forth. These choices, which are not a *match and fit* for them, and therefore, not the right things to be doing, nevertheless serve a highly useful function: They offer momentary pleasure and the knowledge that they are finally choosing with intentionality. The choices are completely controlled by them (even when they are assuming that some disease made them choose food, alcohol, or drugs).

Placating Pain with Poison

Sheila was quite open about her need to remain closed off from the world. She isolated herself from people, was afraid of others, and often went out of her way to avoid the most mundane of situations due to what happened to her last year: attempted rape. She had just boarded a train home from work when suddenly, two men physically accosted her and stole her purse. Witnesses, startled by the event, which required only seconds to occur, gasped in horror, waiting for it to end so they could exhale.

In the months that followed, she was unable to reclaim her purse or her dignity. A single mother, she lived in the shadows of fear, feeling helpless and confused, unable to make decisions in several areas of her life—especially regarding her route to work.

She shamefully hid her smoking (what she calls her "nasty habit") from her ten-year-old daughter, Samantha. One thing she was less successful in hiding was her noticeable weight gain, resulting from her late-night binging. Frequently unable to sleep, Sheila would raid the refrigerator after Samantha had gone to bed, looking for any forbidden sweet she could get her hands on.

The thought that she could inadvertently be passing these awful habits on to her unsuspecting daughter heightened her anxiety, interfering with her sleep and only increasing her cigarette smoking. And yet, she felt powerless to change the deadly course on which she perceived herself to be.

So she sought professional guidance, hoping to free herself from the "ball and chain" existence she was living based on the trauma she had endured. Sheila learned a number of useful things from our sessions: First, keeping your unsuccessful past at the forefront when making decisions is not useful, as you are constantly burdened with all of that baggage. Second, Sheila came to understand that self-medicating—albeit a poor choice—was still a choice. It was her way of feeling in control of her life, as opposed to letting circumstances from the past dictate her actions.

All we needed to do now was substitute something more adaptive for the self-medicating. This came in the form of learning to identify a place inside herself where her entire physical and emotional being came to rest—where it was most balanced and centered. After a while, she found that she could access this calm state on her own—and did! An exercise regimen increased the release of better chemicals than the ones she had been putting into her body—endorphins. And, as a bonus, she also began losing weight. Finally, she learned a way to focus her attention away from what was limiting her, focusing instead on what was possible by picturing and talking about the things she found fascinating. Sheila was then encouraged to make decisions from this physical position, a positive somatic form.

Later in the book you will learn more about how to sustain positive states within your body that will enhance useful decision-making, regardless of circumstances. Among the biggest changes in Sheila's life is that she quit smoking, so there was nothing shameful to hide from her daughter. She still recalled the painful events of her ordeal but made the conscious decision to refuse to let them hamper her lifestyle.

CHARACTERISTICS OF TRAUMA VICTIMS

In many instances, for those who have experienced the trauma of being a victim of a violent crime such as rape, the ability to make decisions begins to diminish, as other people, places, and things become occasions for regenerating the painful memories associated with having been violated. A number of characteristics frequently associated with trauma become apparent:

1. Victims of rape and other violent crimes often believe they have been permanently damaged, and given the choice to have intimate relations with a loved one, may choose to decline. This is a poor choice because it amounts to projecting a painful past into the present and future, where the events that precipitated that past pain no longer exist.

2. Intrusive thoughts, distressing recollections, dreams, and flashbacks often contribute to becoming stuck when having to decide the most trivial of things.

3. It is quite common for such a victim to feel he or she cannot decide to trust other people in a variety of contexts in which that person needs to make a choice that involves those people.

4. In attempting to not think about it, victims may find it hard to concentrate on work, reading, or even simple conversation with friends or peers; instead, they may lose their train of thought so often that deciding anything becomes too burdensome.

5. Still others, feeling out of control, make poor choices such as attempting to regain what they lost in self-defeating ways, by using drugs and alcohol.

PTSD AND DECISION-MAKING

Post-traumatic stress disorder (PTSD) is an anxiety disorder that can develop after exposure to a terrifying event or ordeal in which grave physical harm occurred or was threatened. Psychologists and psychiatrists typically make this diagnosis when symptoms such as recurrent intrusive thoughts, sleep and appetite loss, panic that prohibits movements, nightmares, and other related events persist for more than one month. Traumatic events that may trigger PTSD include violent personal assaults, natural or human-caused disasters such as terrorist attacks, motor vehicle accidents, rape, physical and sexual abuse and other crimes, or military combat.

Those who have been identified with characteristics of PTSD can have trouble functioning in their jobs or personal relationships. Problems associated with PTSD could cause children to have difficulty in school, become isolated from others, and develop phobias. Many people with PTSD repeatedly relive the ordeal in the form of flashback memory episodes, nightmares, or frightening thoughts, especially when they are exposed to events or objects that remind them of the trauma. And, quite understandably, these people often report having difficulty making decisions in their best interest.

A 9/11 Story

Jeremy V. worked on Wall Street. His company had offices in several locations, including One World Trade Center. On the morning of September 11, 2001, Jeremy was to attend the company's monthly meeting there.

But the train from Poughkeepsie to New York City was late that morning. Jeremy never found out why; all he knew was that he was going to be very late—late enough that he would in all likelihood miss the meeting. He tried in vain to call the office on his cell, but the reception was virtually non-existent from the train.

When Jeremy arrived in Grand Central Station, the first tower had already been attacked. Moments later, he heard the violent explosions associated with the plane crashing into the second tower, and the screams all around him that followed. Frantic upon hearing conflicting reports about what had transpired, he desperately attempted to contact his office from Grand Central, to no avail. Power had been interrupted. After several hours of trying to contact members of his firm, he got in touch with a few people from his office that were not from One World Trade, who informed him of the devastating news: Some of his colleagues had perished.

Shaken, bewildered, and confused, he felt stymied—he couldn't decide what to do next. Ultimately, he boarded a train home for Poughkeepsie where his wife was waiting. His feelings of panic—sweating, heart palpitations, nausea, and racing thoughts—had been exacerbated by anticipatory anxiety. He was afraid that his wife would imagine he had become a casualty of the devastating events.

By the time Jeremy sought the services of someone to help him with what were clearly PTSD symptoms, fifteen months had passed. During that time, he had been having difficulty making the most mundane of choices: what route to take to a particular destination, whether or not to shop for something he or his family needed—even whether or not to leave the house, the only safe haven he knew.

The focus of the work with Jeremy was on teaching him to place his attention where he wanted it most, on what was possible for him, rather than on all the pain that sustained his PTSD symptoms. This involved a series of complex interventions, the outcome of which was that he learned to make better internal pictures; to use reassuring, peaceful self-dialogue; and to center his internal feelings in relation to targeted activities and preferences in his life. As this process developed, his sleep patterns improved and his physical panic abated. As his counseling sessions came to an end, he had begun taking his wife out to dinner and finding other desirable reasons to leave the house more often.

Psychologist Roxanne Silver and her associates evaluated the effects of the September 11 terrorist attacks on New York City and Washington, D.C., in a national longitudinal study. Her research focused on the immediate and long-term responses to the attacks, and found that the severity of exposure to the event, rather than the degree of loss, predicted the level of distress among people. For example, people who reported seeing the planes smash into the World Trade Center buildings experienced more PTSD symptoms than average, but people who experienced financial losses because of the attacks did not. Other studies have shown that simply watching traumatic events on TV can be traumatic to some, especially those individuals who had preexisting mental or physical health difficulties, or those who'd had a greater exposure to the attacks.

Being exposed to attacks, of course, transcends 9/11. Many of the aforementioned consequences characteristic of PTSD symptoms are applicable in situations of war.

Combat PTSD and Decisions

Marcus was a supply sergeant with a unit that was part of the first wave of troops to reach Baghdad. On the way, in the town of Karbala, Marcus's unit encountered major opposition. The tank just in front of his was destroyed, and one of his closest army buddies was killed instantly. Marcus watched this doomed soldier as he was engulfed in flames, flailing about in a futile attempt to extinguish himself. A moment later, Marcus took some shrapnel from an explosion nearby. Outmanned by the enemy, it was only by the grace of God that he escaped capture.

An hour later, two more units behind his encountered the same resistance and emerged victorious, saving Marcus's life. For days following this event, he experienced a ringing in his ears; two years later, he still wakes up in the middle of the night on many an occasion in a cold sweat, breathing heavily and feeling heart palpitations. On several occasions he has been at a loss to explain the difficulty he has had making decisions.

Combat troops returning from war have often experienced PTSD. Such individuals undergo a kind of "aftershock" from the events in which they've participated. This occurs as markedly distressing internal experiences (pictures, dialogue, and feelings) replay persistently throughout their daily lives. Many report difficulty sleeping or concentrating; others experience a range of psychophysiological responses such as sweating, shaking, or stomach distress; and many find it difficult to make decisions, which often results in avoiding work or other activities, and withdrawal or detachment from individuals, or even from their own feelings.

Counseling is of significant value to these individuals. There are several different therapy models for treating PTSD:

1. "Systematic desensitization," in which a person gradually becomes able to relax in the presence of anxiety-provoking situations;

2. Hypnotic protocols, to separate and distance trauma;

3. Medications such as strong antianxiolytics and antidepressants;

4. Avant-garde models that help people "rewrite" their pasts by shifting how they represent those experiences internally—visions, sounds, and feelings, for example, the stuff of NLP;

5. And then there is an approach that leans heavily on training an individual to place all attention where he wants it—on what is possible in life, rather than attending to pain.

PTSD is a highly vivid and durable form of trauma that is likely best treated by a combination of several of the above.

TRAUMA, BRAIN ACTIVITY, AND DECISIONS

When faced with behavioral anomalies that may result in difficulty making decisions, it's not uncommon for doctors and research investigators to attempt to locate biological correlates to explain what is being observed as attributable to some disease process. Possibilities may include a mysterious organic lesion, over- or under-active brain impulses, a release of neurotransmitters, or other similar phenomena.

A 2007 study by Victor Carrion, MD, of Stanford University School of Medicine, in conjunction with the Lucile Packard Children's Hospital, examined brain-activity patterns in severely traumatized children and drew comparisons to the brain function of healthy children. Their conclusion was that the traumatized children's brains did indeed function differently from those of the identified healthy children. The researchers used an experimental technique called functional magnetic resonance imaging, or fMRI, to compare brain-activation patterns in sixteen children with symptoms of PTSD with the patterns seen in fourteen age- and gender-matched nontraumatized children as they performed a simple decision-making task. The fMRI technique uses changes in blood flow and oxygenation (which the procedure measures) as a way of detecting neuronal activity or changes in electrical impulses in different regions of the brain. The conclusion they drew from this study was that although the two groups accomplished the task equally well, they used different parts of their brains to do so.

In effect, those with PTSD symptoms showed greater activity in the region of the brain involving emotional awareness, called the *insula*. This is consistent with the characteristic behaviors one would observe in those identified with PTSD, many of which are emotionally laden behaviors.

Furthermore, they opined, people with PTSD often have trouble paying attention and responding appropriately to experimental tasks, perhaps due to heightened physiological arousal arising from their traumatic experience. As a result, many children with PTSD symptoms are diagnosed with attention-deficit hyperactivity disorder, or ADHD. But it's difficult to tell whether the two disorders are truly related, or if they simply have overlapping symptoms. In either case, it is clear that some damage has occurred. This, of course, adversely affects their ability to make useful decisions.

Several things about this study are noteworthy, in this author's opinion.

1. It is an attempt to classify observed behavior as a disease of sorts by identifying an internal, physiological cause—a difference from so-called "normal" children in how much neurotransmission occurs in the regions of the brain (the insula) that would support the researchers' contention of damage. This method is used rather than approaching the observed behaviors as dysfunctional and then seeking to

find ways to simply change them without implying that the children themselves are damaged.

2. What many investigators fail to recognize is that someone's perception of himself/herself as being damaged in some way can exacerbate the observed characteristics that are labeled as disease, and have an adverse effect on the ability to make decisions. There is support for this idea among researchers and other professionals.

    In his book *Healing ADD,* Thom Hartmann indicated that too often, the way children's behavior is framed could be "destructive to self-esteem and demoralizing." Hartmann continues: "By reframing their perspective (away from damage), you give them hope and step into their world in a way which can be transformational." According to Hartmann, there are situations where identifying labels can be constructive, and then there are times that labeling someone as damaged in some fashion can be insidious and destructive.

    In support of the notion that negative labeling is destructive, Dr. Daniel J. Siegel, in his book *The Developing Mind,* indicated that interpersonal experiences, such as perceiving and responding to social situations, shape brain development. He believes the brain circuits responsible for perception in social situations are the same or tightly linked to those that regulate bodily states, modulate emotions, and organize memory and the capacity for interpersonal communication, including making choices. Much of this relates to how genes are "expressed," leading to the production of chemicals (proteins) that ultimately shape responses. But to simplify: The beliefs you have about your ability to perform a certain way (i.e., being successful in your activities), which stem from interactions with teachers, parents, and peers, are strengthened by the neurochemical changes in the brain that occur as a result of having those beliefs, leading to decisions. See the recursive loop here? One thing causes and then is affected by the other. The things we are told about ourselves by others, in other words, generate corresponding chemical activity in our brains that has a powerful effect on what we believe is possible for us—including our ability to decide. Interestingly, in this way, *words* become a form of "neurotransmission." And you could say, *all communication* is a "neurotransmitter."

3. Dr. Carrion and his associates required each of the groups of children to make decisions by pressing a button under conditions explained to them while they were inside a hollow, narrow, noisy tube. In my opinion, this is a serious design-flaw error, despite the fact that the researchers did account for the possibility that *f*MRI tests can leave some people feeling claustrophobic and frightened. (The experience can be particularly difficult for children already struggling with past trauma.) Their accounting for this possibility consisted of attempts to neutralize the children's fears by first introducing them to a "mock" *f*MRI machine prior to being inside the real one. But wait!

Why might this not have made a difference?
Consider that one of the more prominent features
of PTSD is *repeated* intrusive thoughts, nightmares,
flashbacks, and difficulty making decisions over a
long period of time. If merely countering terror by
desensitizing for a short while—the apparent purpose
of the "mock" *f*MRI—were effective, PTSD symptoms
would abate after virtually little intervention. But as
those who work with this condition and those who
manifest it will tell you, that isn't the case. The point
here is that testing the brains of severely traumatized
children by utilizing a procedure (an *f*MRI chamber)—
the very elements of which often induce anxiety in the
most normal of people—in all likelihood increased the
traumatized children's anxiety as well, and that might
explain some of their findings.

4. Lastly, those who design studies to find internal,
    physiological causes for aberrant behavior (including
    difficulty making decisions) in order to develop treatments
    often make the assumption that someone is *irreversibly
    damaged,* and the best that can be hoped for is an
    intervention that can modulate symptomatology. This
    type of a cause/effect relationship has often been applied
    to understanding why people who have experienced some
    form of trauma simply can't decide. On the other hand,
    there are those who believe that trauma is an expression
    that someone holds deeply within his neuromusculature
    that can be reversed by instigating a shift in the body
    posture and patterns of movement.

THE POSITIVE *SOMATIC FORM* AND TRAUMA

Notable individuals like Frederick Matthias Alexander, Moshe Feldenkrais, Thomas Hanna, Richard Bandler, Roye Fraser, and Joseph Riggio have concluded that all experiences, traumatic or otherwise, first show up in your body and are held there in a very specific way, expressed through the neuromusculature as postural shifts, micromuscular movements, breathing changes, eye-accessing cues (meaning the path the eyes follow to retrieve information), and gestures.

This way of representing experience, already introduced as the *somatic form,* serves as a framework for the powerful stories, beliefs, and attitudes—or "myths"—that reside inside of us and make up our lives. Consequently, verbal disapproval, criticism, or replayed flashbacks are also *first expressed somatically.*

The question that arises, then, is "What effect would instigating a favorable shift in the somatic form held by someone with a history of trauma or other life stressors have upon his ability to choose wisely?"

Choices "Held" in the Inhibitory Form

Certainly, it would have made a difference in the life of Daphne Merkin, a novelist, critic, and essayist with a reported history of chronic depression that she elucidated in *The New York Times Magazine* of May 10, 2009, in her article, "A Journey through Darkness." Essentially, Daphne experienced considerable trauma as a child, largely in the form of parental neglect and abuse. Feeling uncertain about the outcomes of any decisions she made, she often opted for indecision, staying home and running a lot of negative internal dialogue about what seemed true for her, such as, "There's no hope—it's too late," and "Give up and go back to bed." The position she likely held within her body accurately reflected the trauma she experienced. Thomas Hanna, in his book, *Somatics,* refers to the position held by those who accumulate trauma as the "red-light reflex," and its features will be elucidated in the next chapter.

This "inhibitory" position she held in her body matched the negative, destructive thoughts and feelings she manifested, which had to do with running her life around the avoidance of problems, and self-medicating with antidepressants and a host of other medications designed to make her feel better.

Holding that inhibitory position and continuing to feel compromised and a victim of her problems, Daphne tried to fix herself by adding these chemical substances. Ultimately failing, she turned to repeated hospitalization as a way of taking a break from the trauma she had accrued in the course of her life. Not knowing what to blame it on—genetics or fate—and certainly not considering life from a framework of what would be possible for her if she had shifted to an *excitatory posture,* with positive outcomes, she continued making poor choices that fit the problem-laden way of life that she followed. Ironically, when hospitalized, she encountered what has been referred to as "iatrogenic illness," in which the treatment causes more problems, leading to more treatment, such as massive doses of antidepressants followed by electroconvulsive therapy (ECT), or "shock therapy," followed by more medication. This cycle continued for a while until she became markedly lethargic and withdrawn, a seemingly endless spiral of deteriorated functioning.

All of this further contributed to her feeling of helplessness and an inability to decide for herself, since she had surrendered her decisions to the caretakers who were allegedly making choices in her best interest.

At the end of the article, Daphne indicated that, having switched her meds to still another antidepressant, Abilify, her depression had stepped back for now, allowing her to move forward with her life, although she lived in constant fear that her depression would return again.

Notice how her decisions were still beyond her control. Why she couldn't decide had to do with this *nominalization* to which she had become a prisoner: *depression*. A "nominalization" is an ongoing, fluid activity—usually a verb or adjective—that becomes converted into an event—a noun. In the process, *acting depressed* (which implies fluidity, movement, and control of decisions on her part) had become "her depression," a stagnant event with a life of its own—one which decided for Daphne.

The Embodiment of Trauma and Indecision

When people live life chained to the trauma they have experienced, holding an inhibitory somatic form in the process, the lives they lead are not their own. And neither are their decisions, which often manifest as indecision—the decision to not decide.

Hans Selye, an Austrian physician and endocrinologist, offers another way of understanding this. He conducted research and wrote over thirty books and more than 1,500 articles on the influence of stress on people's ability to cope, and how this is held within the body in different ways. Generally, the human body is like a road map of the stressors that have been incurred over time, and which most definitely influence as well as become affected by the decisions that are made. We will explore this further in the next chapter.

CHAPTER 7

STRESS AND INDECISION: THE COMPRESSION OF EXPRESSION

There cannot be a stressful crisis next week. My schedule is already full.

HENRY KISSINGER

All behavior is first manifested through the body, as discussed previously, showing up in your neuromusculature, breathing, posture, and eye movements. The various stressors we experience are among the things embodied in this fashion, and the effects this has upon deciding poorly or deciding not to decide will be examined in this chapter.

Stress manifested through the body can also at times function as a signal that primes people into recognizing the most useful of choices in a given situation, as you will soon discover. In either case, much of what occurs in relation to decisions and stress is determined by where you place your attention: on problems, or on possibilities.

STRESS TALES AND INDECISION

"There's so much tension at work these days; I don't know whether I should go to my boss and say something, or just sit tight (literally)."

"Of course you couldn't make up your mind about the floral arrangements, the menu, or the invitation design—look at you!

This thing you're planning is supposed to be the best day of your life, and you're totally stressed out!"

"It's now spring, a great time to put the house on the market. I just can't decide if I should sell or not—where would I go? Besides, look how much stuff I've accumulated over the years. Should I put it in one of those storage units, or should I have a garage sale? Why can't I decide? You know what—just thinking about all these choices is making me anxious."

Stress. Tension. Pressure. Anxiety. Although the first three terms are identified as distinct properties in physics and biology, collectively, they are often used interchangeably as vernacular expressions of internal discomfort that impede the making of decisions.

The stress people identify as affecting their ability to decide seems to impact the process of thinking. Under great stress, there is often a loss of concentration, an inability to perceive new information, hampered short-term memory, and a tendency to recycle negative internal dialogue (often referred to as "worry" or "rumination"). Stress at times seems to constrict the range of choices available, often leaving the affected individuals at a loss to decide. So once again, they decide to not decide. Or at other times, a hasty or poor decision is made.

When Stress Makes Up Your Mind for You

Under stress, the choice many people make is to decide that they have no choice. Ever hear the expression, "I had no choice but to . . ."?

Of late, millions of Americans may feel that they "have no choice but to . . ." Countless people are feeling anxious or stressed by problems specific to their lives today, including economic woes, employment pressures, and issues surrounding raising a family and maintaining a home, to name a few. In an article entitled "Stress" by Barbara Basler, which appeared in the May 2009 *AARP Bulletin* (the magazine of the American Association of Retired People), the author cites some comments made by Dr. Sheldon Cohen, a psychologist at Carnegie Mellon University.

Stress, according to Cohen, "is the perception that you are facing demands that exceed your ability to cope." Basler adds, "Today's economic meltdown is triggering widespread psychological stress, which feeds on uncertainty and dread."

Cohen believes that as people's lives become more unpredictable, they feel less capable of making choices; they have less control over their lives. Of relevance is Basler's point that although the stress response is an instinctual mechanism (which actually first manifests as nerve impulses in the "reptilian" or oldest portion of our brains, the *obdulla oblongata*), this response was originally designed to help humans survive a physical threat. Now, it has morphed into the twenty-first-century version. Today, when our reptilian brains "decide" there is a threat, stress hormones such as adrenaline and cortisol (this is the one that causes you to retain belly fat!) are released, leading to a sudden surge of strength—the "fight or flight" response set. Scenarios that seem to trigger this include job loss, problems paying bills, interpersonal relationship difficulties, and exposure to stories of other people who are experiencing the same.

When your brain makes this decision, glucose levels spike to increase your energy level, and your heart rate and blood pressure increase, so blood is moving faster with greater force to provide muscles with the necessary oxygen to keep this cycle going.

None of this is good for you, and if it persists over the years, it can exacerbate health conditions already present, such as heart disease, atherosclerosis (hardening of the arteries), diabetes, autoimmune diseases, and ulcers.

So it stands to reason that if you can avoid some of the bad-news scenarios such as those having to do with financial challenges and personal relationships, you should be good to go when it comes to making decisions *sans* stress, right? Except it seems that everywhere you turn, there is more bad news.

Language that Triggers Stress

News. That's a highly subjective word, isn't it? People use it in many different ways:

1. "I have news for you. . ." is often designed to elicit a bated-breath feeling in the listener. Just like, "I have to be honest with you. . ."; has anyone ever said that to you and followed it up with something you really wanted to hear— something that generated a sense of calm and joyfulness?

2. "The Evening News" suggests that you will be inundated with a litany of stories about people and things that will do nothing to improve your mood, but instead is designed to increase your blood pressure and anxiety. That's what sells, right? (*Okay, let's tune in and find out what else we have to worry about today.*)

3. "Did you hear the news?" This phrase often positions you, the teller, as a privileged informer, someone in a position of

authority, the giver of knowledge. (*The news is breathtaking, and they heard it from you first!*)

However you experience the term *news*, exposing yourself to situations that compound those feelings of doom can only increase your level of stress.

THE NEGATIVE EFFECTS OF STRESS ON DECISION-MAKING

According to L. John Mason, PhD, a leading authority on stress management and author of *The Guide to Stress Reduction,* when we experience stress, it is common to have several reactions that reduce effective decision-making.

For one, in the course of deliberating alternatives pursuant to a decision, we tend to tunnel in on ideas that are old and ineffective, even if it means ending up at an impasse. This is because in response to being overwhelmed with stress, we often fear the uncertainty that considering new ideas or activities can generate. Our ability to search for alternative useful information becomes compromised—compressed! As Dr. Mason states, "We tend to do things the way we always have done, rather than using new ways or new technologies." So, one way stress can lead to indecision is through the repetitive recycling of useless outcomes—the choices we already know don't work.

Second, when we perceive stress, our ability to sustain a train of thought can become interrupted. Instead, we can succumb to the presence of stress through our internal responses—negative internal dialogue, sweating, heart palpitations, gastrointestinal distress, ticks, shaking within the extremities, and more. In effect, there is just too much internal "noise" distracting us from the task at hand.

Third, as a result of our futile attempts to override the stress that is wreaking such havoc with our decision-making, we can fall more easily into negative self-evaluations, as stress affects our self-esteem and self-confidence. Negative thinking and self-criticism are not useful in moving forward and making self-enhancing decisions.

As Gary Klein noted in *Sources of Power,* stress may affect the way information is processed. He, too, cites similar negative effects of accumulated stressful experiences, including a decrease in the time available to gather vital information germane to a decision; the attentional tunneling, or constriction in the range of information to which we attend (mentioned above); the distraction of our attention from the task at hand; as well as a working memory loss, or, at times, difficulty retrieving events from our long-term memory storage.

Choice "Can"-striction

During the first few years of grammar school, Tess lived in an apartment complex in Jackson Heights, Queens. Common to several buildings was a playground completely encircled by fencing, with shrubs growing in and around it. Inside the mesh of metal and greenery that defined the playground's perimeter were enough kid things to consume her energies all day, and benches for parents to discharge some of theirs through knitting and idle gossip.

Situated randomly throughout the playground were a series of wire-mesh trash barrels, designed to keep the area clean. Each day at approximately the same time, an elderly man dressed in khaki-colored clothing entered the park. He was severely hunched over and carried a large sack across his back—a "ragpicker." His face was a road map of a life steeped in stress—furrowed brow, clenched jaw, and squinting eyes that saw only what was necessary.

He would perform a ritual that included reaching inside each trash barrel and spewing out trash in search of aluminum cans. Finding a few, he would first wipe them on his already-stained shirt, and then place them in his sack. Following this, he then replaced the trash that was removed in search of the cans, and then he moved to the next barrel, repeating this process until he had covered the entire playground. He worked quickly, never looking up, right, or left—just moving from barrel to barrel as if he were tethered to a pulley.

Tess and her friends noticed that for all his work, there were few cans to be found, and he would leave the park with a half-full sack. He seemed to work hard but not smart, as lying within the shrubbery along the fencing of the playground were hundreds and hundreds of aluminum cans! Yet, the ragpicker never picked them up. "Why?" Tess thought.

Relating this story as an adult, the answer dawned on her: It was because he thought he knew where all the aluminum cans were located, and he wasn't going to look elsewhere.

What he lacked, as many of us do, was the ability to evaluate and then choose from an array of options. Dr. Richard Bandler of NLP refers to this as "the law of requisite variety." Essentially, as he defined it, in any system—man or machine—the element with the greatest variability is the controlling element. In other words, the more flexibility one has in his behavior, the more choices that are available, and the greater the likelihood of achieving control in a particular situation.

The ragpicker lacked requisite variety. What he did not lack was the ability to constrict his range of choices when he was under pressure to get things done. In trudging along he appeared very stressed, and ignored what to others seemed obvious.

Incurred stress almost seems to have a mind of its own. Like an ever-accelerating race car, stress seems to be in the driver's seat where making decisions is concerned. And the pedal is to the metal, challenging the bewildered and frustrated individual to take control of the wheel. But as soon as you come to the realization that you have a mind of your own, too, taking that control (or not) becomes a choice you can make.

To that end, can stress ever be useful?

STRESS AND DECISIONS: A FAVORABLE IMPACT

Stress is often thought to impact decision-making by challenging the mind and body to adapt to what has been thrown its way. Stress does not necessarily always have a detrimental effect on decision-making. In *Sources of Power*, Klein also contends that if someone can handle the demands and enjoy the stimulation involved, stress can be welcome and helpful. In other words, stress can be both good and bad. *It is our reaction to stress that matters.*

Klein cites an adaptive use of stress for making decisions called *recognition-primed decisions* (RPD). In the midst of a stressful situation, such as a fire or a search-and-rescue operation, a decision-maker recognizes what type of goal makes sense so that priorities are established. The stimulation, or "workable stress," signals the person as to what to expect next, and also provides typical ways of handling it. In that sense, stress can become a kind of catalyst, converting useful energy toward the realization of a decided-upon action.

Stress Shapes Choices

The effectiveness of a decision-maker under stress depends on his/her capacity to utilize the stress to stimulate or expand awareness, versus being used by it as a compressor of experience. The ragpicker in the previous example chose the latter. Maintaining attention to the details of a rigid routine was arduous enough. The only aluminum cans that existed for him were the ones he found along his planned route.

So much of the time, stress itself can determine the choices we make: physiologically, cognitively, and emotionally. Often these choices, which can seem imperceptible, do not serve our best interests. Stress can lead to errors, poor performance, and bad decisions. However, as noted above, acute stress does not necessarily always have a detrimental effect on decision-making; rather, stress may affect the way information is processed. Some of the changes in strategy we make in response to stress are, in fact, adaptive.

A few examples: A signal from your manager that a particular project is due soon may trigger a call to action, propelling your body and mind into overdrive mode in order to complete the task.

You're playing basketball. Knowing you are ahead, but having witnessed the opposing team making several baskets and closing the score to a one-possession game, the juices could start flowing, powering you to score the next basket.

Your wife is about to give birth. All of your senses become highly tuned to the point of keen awareness, and you execute the necessary tactical maneuvers to get her to the hospital—in record time!

In each of these cases, you likely reduced the information being attended to and processed in response to time pressures and reduced cognitive capacity.

THE "BALL AND CHAIN" OF PROBLEMS

Much of the time, experiencing stress is a choice, and a poor one at that. It's often a decision to place attention exactly where you don't want it! This is the *sorting for* problems, as opposed to possibilities, discussed earlier.

Other times, the presence of stress seems to shackle an individual—freeze him in his tracks—as if he has no choices, either good or bad. Sound familiar? Do you feel like you are chained to the problems in your life? Do you feel that you simply cannot decide? Do emotions get in the way, like frustration, anger, and disappointment?

Richard Bandler of NLP is fond of saying, "Disappointment requires adequate planning." Do you place your attention on events and situations that you anticipate will lead to difficulties, and then feel disappointed when you react with stress? Perhaps you awaken each day and run a litany of diatribes at yourself regarding someone or something that you expect will stress you out at work, or you pay attention to the very people, places, or things that lead you to react most negatively.

Do slow drivers piss you off? Do you let others' provocative comments spark confrontation? Do little details get under your skin—the disarray of your children's belongings, the mess in the kitchen, the seemingly random placement of important items in your home, such as keys? Are you aware of that little voice in your head that is constantly informing you of all the things over which you have no control and keep you tethered to that ball and chain of your problems?

"Good morning, Sue . . . or is it? After all, it is Monday, and you've gotten up ten minutes later than usual. Things will only get worse from here. Count on it. Plan on the water in the shower taking a long time to heat up, and try not to fret as you eat your cereal for breakfast totally dry (since you forgot to get milk last night).

Expect a lot of traffic on the way to work. And your manager, Mr. Birdsell, will probably not respond to your e-mails again to discuss your desire for a raise, since he will be busy catering to someone else. Expect Doreen, that pain-in-the-ass suckup who sits across from you, to hold up the morning meeting while she asks a question just as everyone is ready to break for lunch, in order to predispose others toward her agenda. Feel your heart pounding? Stomach gurgling?"

Why go there? Why place your attention on the very limitations you would prefer not to have? If feeling stressed is a series of choices that so often hampers our ability to make useful decisions, why would we choose to feel it when it makes the very act of choosing itself so difficult? So many aspects of our lives point to the fact that the choice to feel stressed has to do with where we place our attention. Recall the adage of Dr. Joseph Riggio: "Where you place your attention is where you get your result." And then the useful corollary that follows: "Always place attention where you want it most."

What the "Thinker Thinks," the "Prover Proves"

This astute phrase, stated by Robert Anton Wilson in his book, *Prometheus Rising,* illustrates that the mind can be thought of as containing two parts: the thinker and the prover. In effect, whatever we give thought to, we organize our perceptions around to make it so.

Wilson states: "If the Thinker thinks that the sun moves around the earth, the Prover will obligingly organize all perceptions to fit that thought; if the Thinker changes its mind and decides the earth moves around the sun, the Prover will reorganize the evidence. If the Thinker thinks 'holy water' from Lourdes will cure its lumbago, the Prover will skillfully orchestrate all signals from the glands, muscles, organs, etc., until they have organized themselves into good health again."

If you think you will have a bad day, or that the people whose attention you seek will be unavailable, or your children will get under your skin, or you simply will not be able to decide something that you expect to be asked to do, in all cases incurring stress in the process, then, it will be so. *It's where you will place your attention.*

In all walks of life, it seems, many people are highly invested in placing attention exactly where they want it *least*! First, they think about something they would prefer not to occur, and then they go looking for it. Think not? Think again . . .

How often do you acknowledge someone who compliments you compared with how often you respond to someone who insults you? Under what circumstances do you compliment your child for having completed his homework or chores compared with how often you scold him/her when those things are not done?

At times during school, a teacher will decide to call on a child she perceives does not know the answer to her question because he didn't do his homework, just so she can ask, "Sheldon, did you read chapter four last night, as assigned?" And then she can follow up with the proverbial, "Why *didn't* you do your homework assignment?" Though this by no means is an accepted convention, it is not uncommon in terms of what we expect teachers to do.

While we're on the subject, parents often get phone calls or letters home from that same teacher. School personnel typically recognize the very behaviors in kids they would rather not have; they even have a context for this recognition, called "in-school suspension." Tell me, is there a special room in school for kids who *do behave* as expected?

Parents often discipline children in the same manner. Remember the example from an earlier chapter: "Why didn't you clean your room?" What is the true intention such a mother holds for that child? In other words, where would she rather her attention be placed? Of course! She wants to see a clean room. But where does she decide to place her attention instead? The result of her decision is that both she and her child experience stress, and the room remains a mess.

In contrast, what do you suppose would happen if this mother asked her child, "When will you be finished cleaning your room and be ready to go to Carvel for one of those chocolate-covered cones you love (or for a trip to the mall to get that video game you told me Tony has; or to have a sleepover with your friend, Simon)?" And, no, this is not *bribery.* That term is defined in Merriam-Webster's Dictionary as "taking payment in exchange for some illicit, immoral act."

So, until performing chores and doing homework are considered "illicit activities," following these desirable behaviors with some form of recognition is simply a matter of placing your attention where you want it most, and in the process, minimizing the stress incurred by you and your child, so that stress doesn't make up his mind—he does.

People are frequently conditioned to go looking for problems, and to place attention where they *want it least*. Stress is often the by-product of this process. What the thinker thinks, the prover proves. The outcome of perceiving life in this fashion is frequently a poor decision, or no decision at all.

Negatives May Seem Natural . . .

The pervasiveness of this phenomenon, of making decisions based upon the negative—what people don't want to be true in their lives—much more than the positive is supported by a wealth of research. The "Prospect Theory," developed by Daniel Kahneman and Amos Tversky, is a widely accepted descriptive model of decision-making, which states that when it comes to making decisions, people are much more sensitized to negative than positive information. That means that decisions will more often than not be based on the presence of something unpleasant—or its relative absence—more than the possibility of gaining something desirable as a result of a particular decision. Similarly, people will go out of their way to decide in ways that minimize or avoid losses more than ways that lead to some gain. A great deal of evidence indicates that the negativity bias emerges partly because in our society, people are more attracted to negative events than positive ones. Regardless of the reason for the negativity bias, decisions from this position are both accompanied by and increase the presence of stress in a recursive fashion.

Some decision-making research suggests the negativity bias is highly robust and exists within the domain of personal and work relationships. Extensive reviews of research on the negativity bias have been provided by Roy Baumeister and his colleagues and Paul Rozin and Edward Royzman, reported in the journals *Review of General Psychology* and *Personality and Social Psychology Review,* respectively. Their work shows that negative acts have a much greater impact on a relationship than do positive ones.

How many times have you either witnessed or heard of a scenario in which a spouse voices one insult to another, and the "victim" decides to retain that information (literally within his body) and hold it against the other person, regardless of how many compliments or other nice offerings are presented over time? Rozin and Royzman also concluded that these highly robust negative attitudes seem resistant to deterioration, and can be acquired through one single faux pas. In contrast, positive attitudes take a lot more effort to acquire.

This state of affairs can often lead to feeling stuck and choosing to not decide something, or to making poor decisions that may not be in one's best interest—again, under a great deal of stress. There is, however, another choice.

. . . But Attending to "What Works" is More Natural

In his inaugural address, President Obama stated, "Instead of throwing money at problems, it's time to invest in what works." Replace the word *money* with *attention,* and you have arrived at the threshold of change. By following this model, you will become better able to transcend the various stressors in your life and be prepared to make life-enhancing decisions: *Instead of throwing attention at problems, learn how to place it where you want it most.*

So how do you learn to place attention where you want it most so you can make useful decisions? This essential element for making useful decisions will be examined extensively in Part 3 of this book.

An essential question within Part 2 has been, "How did we get here?" Now we must ask, "How have we learned to place our attention where we want it least?"

Well, we haven't always done so. From birth, we are designed for success. Our natural state is one in which we are at our absolute *best*—comfortable, confident, and effective. Dr. Joseph Riggio describes the experiences that lead to this state as the *generative imprint*, a concept first developed by Roye Fraser, and described by Roye Fraser and Ann M. Gardner, PhD, in an article in *Anchor Point*, the international journal for effective NLP communicators. The generative imprint is a way of being that we develop early on in life. Dr. Riggio studied under Fraser, and notes the following:

> *At a very young age something happened for the first time that was a really positive experience for you. At that time you would have been completely absorbed in whatever was going on around you, you would have been in a positive and resourceful frame of mind, and you would have felt settled within your self.*
>
> *A way in which we learn, develop and grow, is by "imprinting" experiences into the very core of who we are. These imprints then remain available to us for the rest of our lives.*
>
> *This means that the first positive emotional experience that you had has been imprinted in you. You'll know this because you'll have found that the positive emotional experience returns whenever the environmental conditions around you are "just right."*

Like this, then, we are capable of deciding in our favor, effortlessly, positively, and comfortably. We make many mini-decisions from infancy—discovering our bodies, attending to interesting objects and people, deciding what to play with—without second-guessing ourselves.

You may recall an essential question that was posed in part 1: "How many young children have serious reservations about going out to play?" How many "normally organized" children (i.e., those without developmental anomalies such as autism, for example) lack the curiosity to explore their environment?

HOW WE SHIFT AWAY FROM OUR IMPRINT

As we struggle to establish independence from our dependent beginnings, moving through adolescence into adulthood, we encounter stress, a by-product of the input of various people and situations that occur during our upbringing. Often, much of this stress is retained for long periods of time, in part due to life's uncertainty.

How exactly does our upbringing contribute to this stress? During the trials and tribulations of growing up, we learn from interacting with significant role models to filter our experiences in ways that do not always serve our best interests, and that deviate from the original generative-imprint experiences (those that inform us who we truly are when at our best). We learn this, not that. In effect, we learn to place our attention here, not there.

Some examples include, "Don't play now; you have to clean your room first"; "Don't watch TV now; you have to do your homework first"; "Don't come in through the front door, go around back—only adult guests come in that way"; "Don't play with your food"; "Don't touch anything in the store; stay by the cart"; "No candy—it will spoil your appetite"; "You can't finish that book now; it's time for bed."

In general, learning to choose this, not that, we inadvertently become conditioned to filter or sort information for problems and ways to try to avoid them. We *sort for* stress, and once we know that it's there, we try to make decisions in spite of it.

In the process of learning how to make choices, and often failing to decide, we learn how to use our natural selves poorly. Practiced through time, this liability becomes effortless and more sophisticated as we continue to live within the problem state. We become better able, in other words, to filter or *sort for* stress, to learn to place our attention where we want it least. After a while, stress just seems ubiquitous—a natural part of life. And the best we are taught to hope for is developing coping strategies to manage it. But then, in order to manage something—stress, for example—what must be present first? Think! Where have we already placed our attention? See the dilemma? The more we think about stress, the more we end up accumulating the very thing we are trying to manage.

SOME FINAL INSIGHTS REGARDING *INSIGHT*

Perhaps at this point you can understand that the notion of looking backwards to gain insight into your stressful or traumatic past is just another illustration of placing that attention where you want it least. For in order to recall something from the past, you are in effect reliving that pain in all its glory. Accordingly, gaining insight about past trauma and stress and how it prevents you from making decisions just does not work. Lots of people have the insight to know that smoking is hazardous to their health. They can even tell you why they smoke: to look cool, or because it calms them when they're stressed, or because their parents did. But knowing these things does not lead to the decision to quit!

Insight alone will not help you understand why you can't decide, or, in the case of this chapter, help you learn to make decisions when you have too much stress in your life. Insight doesn't foster change; neither does focusing on the negative. Making potent decisions that produce change for the better has to do with asking more useful questions. For now, two of those include: "Where do I hold my indecision?" and, "How do I make choices that lead to holding indecision in this manner?" These questions will be examined next.

CHAPTER 8

THE EMBODIMENT OF INDECISION—TRUE TO FORM

People say I'm indecisive, but I don't know about that.
GEORGE H. W. BUSH

You've seen it hundreds of times. In fact, whenever you notice someone holding that certain posture, you recognize right away what they are about to say, just before they say it.

"I don't know."

Try this along with me: Breathe in the manner you would if something suddenly startled you. It begins within the abdomen as a contraction of the diaphragm when you inhale (that "Ahhh!" sound), which creates a vacuum, drawing air through the trachea into your chest cavity, high within your chest. Dr. Richard Bandler calls this "visual breathing," because at the same time this is happening, your eyes move up and to the left (if you're right-handed), as if to retrieve information stored as internal pictures.

In that same instant, notice your head also lifting up and tilting slightly to one side, as some facial muscles tighten. Now, bend both of your arms at the elbow, causing them to move upward along the sides of your torso to a position that is waist high, palms facing out. Then, contract your neck and shoulder muscles while holding your arms at the waist-high position you've just achieved. Notice that the contracting muscles will force the tops of your shoulders upward, as if you're trying to touch your ears. Your eyebrows are often up as well, having moved when your head and eyes lifted. Hey! Keep those palms facing upward—no cheating!

All of this happens a *nanosecond* before you say to yourself, or someone else, "How should I know?" Or maybe, "I have no idea." And of course, "Why can't I decide?"

Are you with me on this posture? It's a posture that communicates uncertainty, confusion, and surrender—the posture of a "victim." It's the posture of someone who either *can* not decide or routinely makes poor choices.

Virginia Satir, a highly regarded family therapist, referred to this as the "placater" position, the palms facing up being the dead giveaway. She is best known for getting clients to recognize the incongruity in their lives (i.e., the mismatch between what their mind is telling them and the signals they are getting from their bodies). According to Satir, someone who uses this "placater" position has little self-confidence and needs the approval of others in order to move forward. He is someone who defers decisions, whose worth is dependent upon the impression he makes.

THE POSITION YOU HOLD—*STUCK*

Indecision—the ability to decide to not decide—begins in the body. Before you are aware of having asked "Why can't I decide?"— or, stating it differently, "I just don't know what to do," the quandary has already represented itself in the neuromusculature of your body. That is, you contract certain muscles, shift your posture in a particular fashion, alter your breathing, and gesture in accordance with the notion of indecision even before you realize and can verbalize, "I can't decide!"

Alexander and the Body-Mind Connection

The idea that behavior, thoughts, and feelings are first expressed within the body has been well documented by some notable people. Frederick Matthias Alexander developed the "Alexander Technique," a hands-on teaching method that encourages all the body's processes to work more efficiently, as an integrated, dynamic whole. A Shakespearean actor who developed chronic laryngitis, he was determined to restore full use of his voice. So he began watching himself when speaking and noticed that undue muscular tension accounted for his vocal problem. He discovered and articulated a principle that profoundly influences health and well-being: When neck tension is reduced, the head no longer compresses the spine and the spine is free to lengthen. He realized that how we think affects the way we act; when we think tense thoughts, such as those that occur when we are having difficulty deciding something, the body constricts in a certain fashion in relation to that thinking.

Today, the Alexander Technique is used extensively as a way of teaching people to hold their bodies in a more relaxed and natural way, which promotes more open and free movement. Interestingly, actors also claim that it helps them to overcome stage fright. It can favorably impact a number of limitations—including fatigue, stress, and hoarseness—by using this muscle-releasing technique that corrects the relationship between head, neck, back, and the rest of the body. Alexander's discoveries and successes certainly have ramifications for the positions held within the body that lead to *indecision*.

Mind-Body Mastery and the "Fourth Way Path"

Mystic and spiritual teacher George Gurdjieff explored the relationship between mind, body, and spirit to develop what he called the "Fourth Way Path," a way of achieving mastery that differs in an important way from traditional Eastern philosophical spiritual paths, such as the way of fakir (for physical mastery), the way of the monk (for emotional/spiritual stability), or the way of the yogi (for control of thoughts).

The first three paths require leaving the confines of an ordinary life, such as going off on a mountaintop someplace or to a retreat, and studying the tenets of that particular path. Their teachings represent the Aristotelian principle of "this or that," introduced earlier. You could either go off somewhere and become aware of your mind, body, and spirit, or remain here and live within the structure of your family, job, and friends.

The *fourth way path,* or "the way of the sly man," as Gurdjieff referred to it, does not require withdrawing from the world as you know it, but can be pursued in the midst of an ordinary life. And instead of working with just the mind, the emotions, *or* the body, it works with *all three, simultaneously.* Gurdjieff claimed it was faster and more efficient than the other ways of achieving mastery. "Mastery" can be viewed here as a way of making many tiny decisions that are life-enhancing, especially the decision to remain *present* or aware of what occurs in each moment. He was among those laying the foundation of the relationship between what we think, feel, and do, and how all of that shows up in our bodies.

How Movement Affects Thought

Perhaps less enigmatic than Gurdjieff, but at least as influential in terms of understanding the connection between mind and body and its effects on behaviors such as decisions, was Moshe Feldenkrais. A European physicist with expertise in a variety of fields, Feldenkrais studied the works of F. M. Alexander, George Gurdjieff, and others to develop what he called the "Feldenkrais Method," a model of understanding how the body influences thoughts, feelings, and behaviors. His method is expressed in two parallel forms: Awareness through Movement, and Functional Integration. The former is presented more didactically, which is to say as a verbal lecture, rather than through touch. Its intent is to make one aware of his or her habitual neuromuscular patterns and rigidities, and to expand options for new ways of moving while increasing sensitivity and improving efficiency. The other form, Functional Integration, is a hands-on procedure consisting of several "lessons" through which people may reconnect with their natural abilities to move, think, and feel.

One of the salient features emerging from Feldenkrais's work is the notion that *all thought involves movement,* and vice versa. We don't often consider how we move when we're thinking or trying to make a decision. But, according to Feldenkrais, every decision we make—good or bad—begins with specific body movements. Feldenkrais had an interesting way of demonstrating this principle. He proposed a test: First, mentally count from one to ten as fast as you can. Then, try to double that speed. It immediately becomes apparent that there's an absolute limit to the speed at which you can count, because when you do so, you are using quick sub-verbal movements (i.e., moving your lips to yourself), and therefore, you can only go from one number to the next as quickly as you can make those actual movements. Theoretically, if sub-verbal movements were not involved, you should be able to accelerate the speed of your counting at an indeterminate rate. The crucial point Feldenkrais makes here, cited by Thomas Hanna in his book, *Body of Life,* is that all human conscious and unconscious experience is physiological. It is organic movement.

Okay, stop here. You're dying to try what you just read, right? I get it. So go ahead—decide to take a break, put the book down, and do the test as Feldenkrais designed it above. You will say, "Wow—my lips actually move when I count! I didn't realize that. I also felt like my breathing sped up, too!" Once you've satisfied your curiosity, you can decide to keep reading this book about decisions. Just pick up from this point when you're ready to continue.

How did it go? Pretty amazing, huh? To continue developing this point, the movement that accompanies thought referred to above consists of micromuscular contractions, postural shifts, head turns, tongue movements, breathing changes, eye-tracking cues, and gestures within the body. When it comes to decision-making, if you are feeling indecisive when faced with a quandary, your ability to decide is already being held internally within your body in some specific ways.

Over time, the movements we make in relation to thoughts, feelings, and behaviors (like making decisions) become *habituated* structures—the body's representation of those mental and emotional activities. "Habituated" means that after a while, they "get comfortable" being there and stay there (like a mother-in-law sometimes does!).

We often don't recognize those somatic (physical) components of our indecision until we experience a headache, muscle tension, or a decreased range of motion in a particular area of our bodies. And then we may mistakenly associate those aches and pains with the stress of having to decide, when in reality they are present just a tad before our realization that we are perplexed over making a decision.

Another way of understanding this is that people often do not pay attention to what they are doing while they are doing it. They are frequently unaware of various movements within the body, stressful or not, because their attention is elsewhere, such as wondering why they can't decide, or if they ever will. The Feldenkrais Method teaches *kinesthetic* (as regards the sense of touch) self-awareness as an integral aspect of the work.

Habituated movements of the body reflect thinking and acting patterns such as decision-making. Muscles that are tensed, restricted, or inflexible can translate into the cognitive impasse you experience when it comes time to make a decision. By learning to sense and then move heretofore fixated or constricted musculature, or by eliminating other tensions in the process, you are increasing flexibility both within the body and in your mind, which can facilitate successful decision-making.

A Lifetime of Defense: The "Red-Light" Reflex

Thomas Hanna, PhD, a Feldenkrais disciple and founder of the field of "Somatics" (his approach to mind/body integration), believed that we have conscious control of nerves and muscles and can therefore combat many problems that we have always accepted as inevitable. This includes fighting against the aging process and combating life's vicissitudes, which often lead to the poor decisions we make (or periods of indecision, when we find we can't make any decision at all). Over time, the choices we make in the presence of stress are represented in our bodies in specific ways. Hanna called one of these the "red-light reflex." This is a protective response to events that we perceive to be negative or threatening, ranging from the mere anticipation of something we expect, accompanied by anxiety, to traumatic experiences or events that offer real danger. It is a withdrawal response in neuromuscular form: a decision we make in the presence of stress, albeit a poor one. There are several typical features of this reflex that will seem familiar to you. Overall, imagine the posture of someone mere seconds after being hit in the chest with a basketball he failed to catch. Picture the contraction of the chest and abdomen, along with these other features:

1. "Worry lines" in the face that are the product of many decisions made under stress. This is commonly achieved by contracting the muscles of the forehead and those around the eyes.

2. The muscles at the base of the neck contract mightily in order to support the burden of a thrusted-forward head, which moves this way often when having to decide in the presence of anxiety. As someone makes this head-thrust movement over and over, the neck muscles become stronger and larger, and fat tissue grows around that area of the neck, causing the familiar "dowager's hump." How many people have you witnessed in your life walking around with that thrusted head and hump between their neck and shoulders? Did you just think to yourself, "Oh, *that's* where that comes from; I thought it was just a sign of old age."

3. More decisions in the presence of stress or trauma are exemplified in the red-light reflex by the lifting and rounding of the shoulders. This was the "I don't know" and "Why can't I decide?" posture alluded to earlier. If serious

worries impact someone's behaviors early enough in life, stooped shoulders will occur at a relatively young age.

You will often hear indecisive people report that they have chronically sore necks and shoulders. Accompanying this stooped posture is shallow breathing, as there is a contraction of the abdominal muscles, and the trunk is pulled into a kind of flexed curve, like a bow, the outside of which is represented by your back. In short, people who adopt the red-light reflex have more difficulty breathing, as well as many other maladies commonly linked to the accumulation of stress inherent to old age. This is due to the negative effects of contracted abdominal muscles on the entire viscera. Frequent urination, indigestion, high blood pressure, and gastrointestinal disorders are also common, leading to the need for further decisions in pursuit of relief, often to no avail.

Getting Comfortable with Discomfort

This again is *habituation*—a learned pattern of physical responses within the body that represent the many dilemmas people face when they decide poorly, or can't decide at all.

In 1981 Moshe Feldenkrais published one of his landmark works, *The Elusive Obvious*. The basic premise of the book is that the negative attitudes and behaviors people manifest are so ubiquitous, they often go unnoticed—yet they appear somatically in posture, muscle tension, and gait, and may eventually lead to death.

What types of decision dilemmas might people embody in this way? Perhaps they have a family and are busy taking care of the kids; they also hold down a job that may be in peril, putting a strain on their ability to pay the bills; they have relationship difficulties; they are not sure about purchasing a big item. Any of these or other life problems can be held within the body in a negative way. The physical responses associated with decision-making are highly adaptive, meaning they ingrain themselves into the functional patterns of the central nervous system. This means, essentially, that they get there—and stay there!

This happens because these somatic features accumulate through time and then give rise to still other poor decisions (or "no decisions") as life continues. Gurdjieff believed that "people go through life asleep." Hanna lends support to this comment in stating that many people experience "sensorimotor amnesia." This is a way of describing the disconnection we experience with our bodies as a result of disuse. What the brain cannot sense, it cannot move.

When the choices we make habituate in our bodies in such a fashion that we feel discomfort, we will either become indecisive in relation to a future activity, or select poorly in that regard, thereby compounding the negative physical effects that occur throughout the body.

Have you ever felt neck or shoulder stiffness after an encounter with an employer, or hours after having reprimanded your child for some misbehavior? You may decide that it's better to remain immobile with ice packs or ointment on the affected area. Subsequent to this experience, you may elect to go easy and avoid stretching or free-swinging movements so as not to cause further injury. And so that stiffness becomes further ingrained and less likely to abate. This physical manifestation, then, has a direct effect on restricting the range of choices you will consider, mentally, when it comes time to make a decision.

In that same vein, someone who is already suffering this type of discomfort may be consumed by indecision when offered an opportunity to partake in an event or adventure, fearing that "in her condition," all that walking might do more damage than good. Then, her range of motion will likely continue to decrease, leading to more decisions that further limit her body. Someone who perceives himself as being constantly under pressure, incurring frequent headaches, may decline the opportunity to get away and enjoy a concert, movie, or Broadway show, fearing the possibility that "all that commotion" may induce a headache.

Ironically, according to Hanna, the very act of reestablishing a sensorimotor connection in a particular muscle group—in other words, increasing flexibility of movement—is more often than not the better decision!

SENSORY INFORMATION AND DECISIONS

Just as the sequence of numbers you press on your phone leads to the person you want to speak to, there is a sequence of internal sensory experiences—primarily visual, auditory, and kinesthetic—that when "dialed up" leads to a particular decision. On the other hand, sometimes that sequence of events leads to a kind of "wrong number"; instead of producing a good decision, the string of sensory data occurring as recycled bad thoughts or feelings leads to a poor decision. You know, like that little voice running in your head upon awakening, discussed earlier, which can have you already deciding things will work out badly today.

Richard Bandler, codeveloper of Neuro-Linguistic Programming (NLP), had this to say about making poor decisions in his book, *Get the Life You Want*: "Getting over bad thoughts is an important part of the process. When you think bad thoughts, you feel bad. When you feel bad, you will make bad decisions."

For Bandler, how decisions manifest within the body is somewhat different. One of the tenets of NLP is that people create a series of internal sensory experiences—visual, auditory, kinesthetic (feeling)—that lead to external behaviors. Each of these sensory experiences contains qualities or characteristics that further clarify them, called "sub-modalities." For example, visual sub-modalities would include the number of images; whether they are moving or still; the size, shape, and color (or lack thereof, if they are black and white); whether the images are bright or dim, bordered or non-bordered; and whether they are "associated" (you're in the picture you visualize and see what you would normally see out of your own eyes) or "dissociated" (you see another "you" in the picture created by your "mind's eye"). Auditory sub-modalities would feature volume, pitch, tempo, tonality, the direction sound is coming from, and rhythm, to name a few. And kinesthetic sub-modalities are things like location within the body, temperature, breathing rate, pressure, and weight.

Try it. Consistent with my belief about the difference between *being* and *doing,* having an experience of something makes a deeper, more lasting impression, and more often leads to a desired outcome when it comes to making a decision, than does merely reading about that something. So go ahead: Think about the last movie you enjoyed, or a romantic encounter or exciting event in which you participated. Picture what you saw back then, and be sure to include as many of the visual qualities as you can. Also, tune into any sounds, and get in touch with whatever you were feeling then. Notice the sub-modalities of the sounds and feelings as well. Is the picture moving? In color? Do you see another *you?* Are there voices? If so, coming from what direction (in relation to your current physical space); behind you, from the side? Did you get a particular feeling inside? Where did it seem to start from (what part of your body)?

Bandler's distinctions between making good and poor decisions begin with differences in the way you represent these internal experiences. This is unique for each individual. For example, a poor decision for you may be represented by an internal picture appearing a certain way and in a particular location in space (out in front of your face, to the side, behind you), possibly accompanied by sound and feeling with their corresponding sub-modalities. A good decision will have a different representation.

The internal experiences form a kind of pattern for either type of decision, good or bad. The key to understanding the pattern of a good or bad decision is to track what internal experiences lead up to it. If you continue to process information in the pattern that for you leads to bad decisions, you will continue making bad decisions, irrespective of the situations in which those decisions occur. This pattern within your body will dictate the quality of your decisions regardless of whether they are about things like, say, wearing clothing inappropriate for the weather conditions, or choosing a "big-ticket item" such as a car, house . . . or spouse!

NLP and Indecision

Within the context of NLP, *indecision* (as opposed to making good or bad decisions) has to do with something else. Recall that the internal sensory experiences that lead to external behaviors—i.e., those that comprise making a decision—occur in a unique sequence, one following the next, sort of like a telephone number. First one thing happens, say, an internal picture, and then perhaps some internal dialogue about that picture, followed by a feeling.

The last sensory experience that occurs prior to a decision is your *criterion* that allows you to exit that internal sequence of events. So again, if the sequence of events were a phone number, that last criterion input would be followed by a ring. Each person organizes this sequence differently. Some, for example, may first have a little internal dialogue, which then calls up the picture, followed by an internal feeling; others may begin with the feeling and end with a picture, and so forth. The entire sequence where decisions are concerned is referred to as a "decision strategy" in NLP parlance.

By illustration, here it is, a holiday weekend. You are invited to a barbecue and asked to bring dessert. In considering your decision as to what to purchase, you might first picture the number of people who will also attend, just to get a total in mind. Then tell yourself, "Sally and Doug both like cannolis—he says the cream makes it—and the Renaissance Bakery here in town has the best cream around. But Jack's wife Suzanne is overweight, and very sensitive to things like that. He told me during the Yankees game we were watching that she eats a lot of fruit lately. I like chocolate, but Phil is allergic—and so is his son." So far, no decision has been made. Notice that no internal feeling (in this instance, the criterion for making the decision) has been reached—yet.

So let's say you then picture an open-top fruit pie with custard and sprinkles. "It's got custard made from that good Renaissance Bakery cream," you tell yourself, "so that will satisfy a number of people. And it has a lot of fruit that people like Suzanne can pick at." Then, suddenly, you get a warm, relaxed internal feeling in your abdomen that signals the choice point has been reached. You exit from this strategy and decide to get the pie.

Getting a Busy Signal

Indecision occurs when these internal sensory-experience components of your decision strategy don't keep moving along toward a conclusion, to that "choice point" criterion. Instead, some of those internal sensory experiences just keep battling back and forth, creating what we call "looping." In our phone example, those internal experiences, having been "dialed in," would lead to a rapid busy signal—the kind that indicates a technical problem—before you even get a chance to enter the criterion sensory experience and then get a ring. In essence, there would be no decision.

The TOTE Model and Decisions

Another way to understand this process of indecision from the framework of NLP is to consider the concept known as "TOTE." The acronym stands for "test, operate, test, exit." This model, created by Eugene Galanter, Karl Pribram, and George Miller, offered an alternative schema to the strictly Stimulus-Response (S-R) theory of psychologist B. F. Skinner. The issue at hand concerned how people respond to the environment in which they live. These psychologists were basically implying that rather than seemingly automatic responses—reflexes in the presence of certain events, as Skinner believed—responding involved some conscious decisions. An NLP associate of Richard Bandler, Robert Dilts, incorporated the TOTE model within the structure of NLP to explain the internal sequence of events that leads to external behaviors, such as making decisions.

Let's take the decision "My hair is now combed to my satisfaction" as an example. (To make this realistic, we will need to picture someone other than me, given that hair combing is no longer a major part of my life.) So let's picture a woman combing her hair who may wish to achieve a specific look: straight, smooth, silky, falling softly about three inches below her shoulders, and curling under at the ends all the way around, with bangs in the front. That picture would be the desired outcome. So she combs, pulling on the snarls while simultaneously spraying her hair with a product that causes the hair to relax, untangle, and lose its static electrical charge. She looks in the mirror and, likely without realizing it, tries to match what she is looking at to the internal picture she has in her head of how a "finished hair comb" should appear. This is the *test* portion of the process. She may then comment, "Hmm . . . better on the left, but those damn hairs on the right keep flying out and just won't stay in place." She continues combing her hair, spraying it again—this is the *operate* portion—while also listening for a diminished static electrical charge running through her comb, indicating a smoother, softer look.

Notice here what Bandler refers to as "synesthesia," or how a specific sound (i.e., lessened static charge) can relate to a smoother look. We often use synesthesia to explain our experiences, and it is essentially when one sense modality is used to describe another. Other illustrations include having an "intense" experience (a feeling) that you describe as being "bright" (a visual quality); feeling a particular image in different parts of your body; or associating a particular color with the experience of temperature—i.e., red-warm, blue-cool, and so forth. Bandler and his associates suggested that synesthesia, or the overlapping of internal sensory data, makes an experience stronger. This would hold true for making decisions as well. Back to the example . . .

Once again the woman compares what she's looking at in the mirror to her desired internal image—the second *test* portion of the TOTE model. If they match, she gets a feeling—maybe a tingling in her cheeks, or a relaxed feeling within her abdominal muscles—that says, "Stop combing; you're finished." She decides her hair has achieved the desired look, and she stops combing—the *exit* portion of TOTE.

The same paradigm applies when you are hammering a nail or trying to decide what to wear, to eat, to purchase, or to do.

Within this framework, then, indecision occurs when, having created a sequence of internal experiences, for some reason you fail to generate the criterion that will allow you to exit from that decision strategy. So nothing you hold up to yourself in the mirror "feels right," and you can't decide what outfit to wear to work that day. All the SUVs you looked at, regardless of the make or model, look about the same to you, and you don't feel comfortable purchasing any of them. Nothing on the menu jumps out at you, and you tell yourself you don't seem to see anything there that you have a taste for, and so can't decide what to order for dinner. So instead, you keep looping, alternating between *test* and *operate,* as a decision just doesn't seem imminent.

Are you still with me? So far, what you should be getting is that indecision—the ability to decide to not decide—and poor decisions begin within your body and are held there as specific patterns in your neuromusculature. But what drives us to adopt these representations in both our bodies and minds that comprise making decisions?

Surely, you are familiar with the expression, "It just feels right," or "I'm comfortable with that choice." On the other hand, how about, "It just doesn't sit right with me"; "This is all making my head spin"; "I don't see myself doing that"; or, "It leaves a sour taste in my mouth"? These are expressions that reflect how elements of decision-making are impacted by our bodies. And this happens both when we are successful and unsuccessful in making a decision. However, the choice between choosing well or poorly—or not at all—has to do with something else in addition to the specific sensory patterns within our bodies.

DECISIONS AND THE DIRECTION OF ATTENTION

According to Dr. Joseph Riggio, architect and designer of the Mythogenic Self™ Process, where we are taught over time to place our attention has a powerful effect on our decision-making. To review a bit, Dr. Riggio's position is that the life you are experiencing in relation to making choices—*deciding*—is determined in large part by where you place your attention. Recall that people who are typically stuck and can't seem to decide, or those who make poor decisions, often place their attention where they want it least. In the process of doing so, they assume an inhibitory somatic form (body position), which by now you know is made up of micromuscular contractions, breathing changes, postural shifts, gestures, and eye movements. This somatic form is a reaction to the *problem state* they are living out of, as described in a previous chapter. They hold this inhibitory form as opposed to making decisions from an excitatory somatic form, one in which micromusculasture, breathing patterns, postural shifts, eye movements, and gestures reflect possibility—what is "working" in one's life. Consider one man's experience:

A Back-Handed Proposal

"Should I ask Laura to marry me? Life as a single man can get lonely, and there are many times I long for someone—after work, on weekends—to share my life. It gets pretty ugly at times, I know, but . . . well, I mean, sure, we've been dating for about a year. She seems attentive, but then, maybe she acts that way because she feels sorry for me. We like many of the same things; we agree politically, emotionally, and spiritually on a host of subjects, but those are all trivial things. What if we're not compatible, sexually? What if she doesn't find me attractive? What if she says no? I guess the worst thing that can happen is that I'll still be living alone. It kind of stinks, but it's not that bad—I can always get a dog . . ."

This is an example of deciding from an inhibitory frame (one that first and foremost is organized around problems and their avoidance), and is typical of those who decide by worst-case scenarios. In contrast, deciding from the excitatory frame (one organized from the position of what is possible—what "works" in life) can render a different scenario.

A BETTER CHOICE

"Should I ask Laura to marry me? My heart races when I hear her voice on the phone, and more so when we meet for an evening or day out somewhere. She seems to fit like a glove—I can anticipate her moves and she mine after having dated for almost a year. I know I love this woman: The feeling is one of electricity in every cell of my body. She takes my breath away—I can hardly wait to surprise her, or make her laugh about something that happened when we were apart, or share a stimulating story or event from the day's activities. I can envision the excitement in her voice as we return from our honeymoon and she goes about the business of setting up our new home. I guess asking her to marry me is a no-brainer; the only question is how I can truly surprise her in the process."

As a woman, from which guy would you rather receive a proposal (even if your answer were to be "no")?

When you live life from inside a box called the "problem state," everything you decide is considered from within that framework. Your every decision is mainly in relation to the impact it will have on a particular problem, which just drives the negative somatic form you express even deeper. This is how the red-light reflex, described by Hanna, becomes habituated.

Living inside the world of problems is not a natural state. It's something we learn and then ingrain within our neurology. As part of living inside problems, people project past situations in which they've been unsuccessful into the present as things to watch out for ("away from" motivation).

"Should I go out with him? He's a lawyer, and I dated one two years ago. What a nightmare—the guy challenged everything I said. I was exhausted by the end of the night, every time we went out. Lawyers . . . ugh! I don't know—I just don't want to get into another round of constant debating again. Why can't I decide?"

This sort of thing frequently generates conflict, the kind that gives rise to indecision. But the elements of indecision go much deeper than this . . .

INTERNAL AND EXTERNAL FRAMES OF REFERENCE

Dr. Riggio believes that indecision arises from the conflict between our highly regarded, positive, somatic responses—the internal body position that's held, and represents what we know to be most true for us when we are at our "best" (sometimes referred to by Riggio as one's *center*)—and the intellectualized input we get from others, which serves as an external frame of reference. This input is offered as advice or commands, and we often follow it to avoid problems (i.e., *Do this so that something bad won't happen*).

During my interview with Dr. Riggio, an international business consultant, teacher, and coach, he stated, "People become indecisive because the way they make decisions is based upon a number of flaws that they operate out of. One of the flaws is that instead of making decisions based on what, for them, is true, coming from their center, they make decisions as a result of what others have told them should be true."

In this way, decisions are not based upon what someone believes is a "match and fit" for him, what he knows to be true within him, but rather, upon what has been foisted upon him by outside sources; that is, what should be true. As a result, this individual will often have difficulty holding that highly regarded internal body position intact when he makes a particular decision based on this external information, because he doesn't believe it himself.

And so, his excitatory, highly regarded body position deteriorates into an inhibitory one, having "caved in" to external pressure. (Ever wonder where that expression comes from?)

Going with His Gut

Cameron was an athlete who possessed uncanny skills. He played baseball in high school, and then at the minor league triple-A level. As a second baseman, he had catlike quickness—he turned more double plays than anyone in the league. At the plate, that quickness served him well, as he also hit safely more times than any of his teammates. Cameron set team records for triples, steals, and runs batted in—all in the same season! And to think all of this might not have happened if he had listened to his high school guidance counselor, Mr. Witherspoon, who wanted him to pursue a career in engineering. That counselor implored him: "Cam, you got the highest possible grade of anyone in your math class. And you did almost as well in all your science classes, except biology. Your calling is to apply those skills in a field where you can create something for others. You really need to apply to colleges that specialize in preparing you for a career in engineering. Now, in the interest of saving you some time, I put together a list of colleges that will get you there . . ."

When Cameron was on the ball field, a certain calmness came over him—as he explained it, a feeling of belonging. His senses, especially his sight, grew sharper. The world seemed to grow silent, as he described it, while everything slowed down so he could catch up to it—hitting, fielding, and running to steal a base. He was at his best.

From time to time, thoughts of Mr. Witherspoon would pop into his head and he would remember how emphatic that guy had been about Cam becoming an engineer. And when Cameron thought about it, imagined giving up baseball, obtaining an engineering degree, and getting a job with a firm or possibly the government, everything grew fuzzy. He would develop a pit in his stomach and would lose his concentration. "Good thing that this didn't occur to me at the plate!" he thought.

How We End Up Choosing Badly

Riggio notes that when a person's natural, internal response to the decision doesn't match what he has been told the decision should be, there is a conflict between what he thinks is supposed to be true and the signals he is getting internally about how he understands the world to be for him.

Now, instead of being able to navigate successfully around this dilemma, for example by saying to himself regarding a decision, "Okay, I hear what others are telling me, but I'm going to stick with my gut,"—which is to say, pay attention to the somatic signals he gets from his body—he may too often rely upon an intellectual process, trying to make sense of the stuff being foisted upon him as a way of deciding. Why he may do this will become apparent momentarily. But in any event, the difficulty is that this intellectual process is completely out of sync with his physical, somatic responses—his body, his gut, and his intuition. Therefore, he is internally in conflict and as a result, becomes indecisive.

In other words, in a given situation, he could ask himself, "Is this thing I have to decide a match and fit for who I truly know myself to be within my body, at the deepest level?" If the answer is yes, this would be in sync, and he would still be able to hold that somatic position around making this decision. Too often, the intellectual process—the input he receives from others about what should be true—is not in sync with his somatic experience, so the answer to this rhetorical question becomes emphatically, "No."

In order to discover the somatic form for who you truly know yourself to be, you need to learn how to pay attention to your body in specific ways that will be presented in greater depth in part 3 of this book. Then, as choices come up, they will either be a match and fit, allowing you to retain that highly regarded form as you make a decision, or not. If you discover that some external input is not a match and fit, and yet you still choose this particular option, you will be pulled out of that highly regarded form, assume an inhibitory body position, and experience distress.

In the situation above, you would think that having noticed this mismatch between the external input from his guidance counselor and who he most knows himself to be, Cam would have made a decision based on his natural instincts. But wait. There is a complication brewing . . .

Essentially, he is of two minds about things. So, rather than being able to come to an easy resolution for himself about what he believes or holds to be true, he is in conflict because his own internal life experience (his somatic expression, within his body) suggests one thing, and yet, all of his intellectualization and learning is suggesting something else. Cameron was able to hold his natural internal state—calm, but sharp and quick—around the decision to become a ballplayer. But it was more difficult to hold this form within himself when considering information from outside that he should have pursued a degree in engineering. The latter caused a good deal of internal distress or conflict.

Here's the complication to this dilemma: The intellectual input contributing to a decision—the stuff that has been inculcated in him that should be true—is the very thing that is often rewarded by society. So there is a kind of approach/avoid component. On the one hand, he could have decided in favor of what he's been told would result in recognition or approval (engineering); but if he'd done so, he would have ended up feeling bad, because opting for that particular choice was not a match and fit for who he is, or what he knows is most true for him (which registers within his body).

Choices That Lead to Conflict Through Time

Another larger, more comprehensive example will suffice to make the points elucidated here.

Let's begin with childhood. The typical childhood experience is one where going outside to play is important. We are naturally designed for success, and a good deal of that arises from our ability to explore our environment as a way of learning about the world. Children live in the moment, making it possible for them to use their senses to soak in as much new information as possible.

Animals are exquisite at this as well, by the way. So much of what we learn comes from observations about how they navigate their world at their "best," placing attention on enjoying the moment during their explorations.

So the instinctive response of a young child—what his body is telling him to do—is to go outside and play. It's a beautiful day, the sun is shining, he can smell the fresh scent of newly mown grass and hear birds singing, and there's a ball game waiting to happen. But there is a precedent given to him: school. This is what he is supposed to be doing. After all, he's no longer four; he's eight. So now he finds himself locked in a classroom, sitting up straight; waiting to be recognized before speaking, following the instructions of this adult assigned to be his surrogate parent for six hours per day, the teacher; and in general, being compelled to do what in no way matches those instinctive urges of childhood.

As a reward for ignoring what his body is telling him to do (that natural desire to be part of the beautiful outside world) and responding instead to what the teacher is offering him (meaning, he has to pay attention and respond, speak only when recognized, and remain in his seat), he will receive gold stars, good grades, and a promotion: the opportunity to do this all over again, for ten years or so, leading to still more opportunities to seek the approval of others.

John Taylor Gatto, an award-winning New York City teacher whose experience has spanned three decades, stated in his latest book, *Weapons of Mass Instruction,* that *education* differs from *forced schooling.* Education occurs from the inside outward. It is about exploration that leads to self-awareness and self-mastery. Schooling operates from the outside in, and is a matter of habit and attitude training—training that is often out of sync with our own instinctual responses, and designed to serve all the "should-be-trues" of others. The major contention of his book was expressed superlatively in a poem he wrote for his granddaughter, Kristina:

> *Whatever education is*
> *it should make a girl unique,*
> *not a servant.*

It should give her courage
to tackle the big challenges, to find principles which
will serve as a guide on the road ahead,
make her strong in the
presence of evil,
let her love her fate whatever it is.
Above everything, it should lead her to discover
what really matters:
how to live and how to die.

In the course of making decisions, this is an essential aspect of how we learn to distort and override what seems most natural to us, most "true"—very often as early as childhood—in favor of what we have been taught by the significant people in our lives, and by mass media. In effect, we succumb to the servitude of others and their intentions, as Gatto might conclude.

Back to the example: Fast-forward this distortion twenty or thirty years. There has now been a huge buildup of these experiences—occasions in which someone has had an opportunity to do one thing, which is highly consistent with his instinctive urges, and yet in order to survive in the world, he has had to override those urges and do what he is told. In essence, he has been rewarded for learning to do what he is told rather than what he truly wants to do. By going against his natural inclinations in service of what is expected, he has learned that he will receive personal recognition or increases in salary, among other things. Keep in mind that our society is designed to offer rewards when people are willing to subjugate their natural desires for those of their superiors.

The consequence on a large scale is that while we may experience great dissatisfaction in life, at the same time we continue to reap great rewards for having sacrificed our intuitive sense in favor of society's preferences.

Examples of the disparity between your gut—what's true for you—and what's being foisted upon you by others are ubiquitous, so much so that as you read this, you may be able to list decisions that seemed natural for you and those that seemed uncomfortable, foisted upon you by others against the grain of your highly regarded somatic form. Perhaps you wanted to purchase something that happened to be on sale, but your spouse convinced you not to, and shortly thereafter, you regretted not having done so because the price had now gone way up. Or, at one time, you might have experienced both fascination and facility with your science courses in school and found it highly desirable to pursue a career in medicine, but then sacrificed this natural inclination in service of what else was requested of you: your needed presence in the family business. Then, years later, you may have felt regret for having decided to work in a capacity that for you seemed to not be the right thing to be doing.

Consider a time you were driving someplace new without the benefit of GPS. Your instincts might have guided you along a certain path when suddenly, perhaps a friend or loved one sitting next to you strongly suggested you alter the route. "Don't go that way! Turn here; I know a shortcut." Ever hear those words? If you succumbed, your gut might have tightened a bit—especially if in the end your instincts were correct.

Your Frame of Reference and Indecision

There is a disparity between the mind and body inculcated from early childhood right on through adulthood. At some point, many people are forced to acknowledge the disparity because the physiological responses that are being generated by their bodies as a result of acquiescing to these external forces have reached a point where they cannot be ignored. Those who believe that making a decision from this external-evaluation position is inevitable, despite it not being a match and fit for who they truly are, wind up feeling bad.

"Take this job," you are told, "and you will get paid very well." And you will. But you may also experience great dissatisfaction in your life and, as a result, slowly and insidiously incur a number of symptoms, which could include headaches, chronic fatigue, stress ulcers, eczema, and muscle tension. This is the cost of making decisions that are a total mismatch with who you truly are.

As it becomes increasingly more difficult for someone to override these body signals, to withstand all the symptoms and do what others have told him to, indecision often results.

"I'm sick over this"; "The thought of being in that boardroom with some of those characters is making me nauseous"; "My heart aches every time I think about moving"; "I don't know. I feel like my head is stuck in a vise every time I have to go to one of those hardware trade shows and schmooze over boards and nails." These are all examples of what can happen when the aforementioned disparity grows large enough to reach a point of indecision.

Not uncommonly, indecision can lead to making poor decisions. Indecision is uncomfortable to many people. In the process of trying to resolve their discomfort, they will turn to several forms of self-medication: alcohol, drugs, cigarettes, gambling, sex, or food.

What happens is that when people spend years living out of balance with themselves—that is, when they are forced to consider making choices that are not aligned with who they truly are—as previously described, one of the ways they seem try to reconcile this inconsistency is by doing other things in which they perceive that they are free to exercise their desire for immediate pleasure, even if they know the end result will often be injurious to themselves—or others. The perception behind such poor decisions is that the immediate pleasure of doing what they want that feels good is a welcomed respite from constantly having to do what they don't want to do, which makes them feel bad. For even though these choices may not be in their best interests, they are consistent with the desire for a sense of peace, pleasure, comfort, or stimulation, experienced internally, and are therefore *true to form*.

WHERE CAN YOU GO FROM HERE?

So indecision, as well as decision-making, is first expressed in the body and held there in specific ways. As some notable people have demonstrated through their work, there is a connection between the position you first hold and what you then think and feel, and these bear a direct relationship to what you *can* or *can not* decide.

Typically, when faced with indecision or after having selected a poor choice, people want to know why. Often, they will postulate a connection between some negative events in their history and their current predicament, holding a highly inhibitory somatic form in the process. At times, they will recognize that a particular choice didn't seem natural but had been foisted upon them through the input of others. In any event, facing this dilemma, lots of folks end up placing their attention exactly where they do not want it to be: squarely in the middle of a landscape of problems.

"So, how do I move from making poor decisions or just being indecisive to making good decisions—those that are truly in my best interests, and which are aligned with who I most know myself to be?"

It's time to explore a different landscape: the landscape of possibility. In so doing, I will take you on a journey along the road less traveled—one that rises above adversity and leads you to the choices that best suit your needs.

PART THREE
MAKING EXQUISITE DECISIONS

CHAPTER 9

AN ALTERNATE UNIVERSE

Once you make a decision, the universe conspires to make it happen.

RALPH WALDO EMERSON

We don't respond directly to incoming information from the environment. We first run it through a series of "filters," then act in response to that filtered information, which represents how we perceive it to be. This process of *filtering* incoming data occurs before we even recognize it as something that will require decision-making on our part. The filters are our sensory modalities—visual, auditory, kinesthetic, and olfactory/gustatory—through which we pay attention to different kinds of information.

The filtering process has a significant impact on the experience being perceived. We will examine how decisions are affected by the filters we use to sort for the things that work in our lives compared with those that cause us difficulties. As you will soon discover, this filtering process affects every aspect of decision-making, from the body position that is held in that moment through the cognitive, emotional, and behavioral aspects of an actual decision.

We live in two worlds when it comes to decision-making: One contains a vast universe of those who makes choices based on the idea that anything is possible. These people orient themselves toward what I call an *excitatory bias,* reflected both by the highly positive position they hold in their bodies when they are at their best, and where they place their attention, which contributes to their overall physical and emotional well-being. That is, they *notice for* potential, purpose, utility, strength, and achievement. They perceive their universe as *benevolent.*

The other world (to which many of us belong for much of our lives) focuses on the limitations that exist: the flaws and problems. Those who dwell here operate from an *inhibitory bias*—a compromised body position coupled with attention that is focused on what is *not* working, or that which limits them. They see their universe as *malevolent.*

THE EXCITATORY VS. THE INHIBITORY BIAS

We are naturally designed to achieve what we desire in life, which means we are born sorting our experiences from an excitatory bias. In these instances, *bias* refers to how we organize the particular set of filters through which we experience the world. Recall that we filter information through our senses—visual, auditory, kinesthetic, and olfactory/gustatory. In the broadest sense this organization allows us to sort information for either what is working or what is not working.

Neither bias is "true" in that your body sensations, beliefs, feelings, and behaviors operate on incoming data through one or more of these filters. So why is there no truth? Consider that two people experiencing the same incident (each using his own filters) can interpret it in vastly different ways. One person navigating a canoe down a river will come to a section containing rapids and immediately think, "Nature is magnificent and exciting! I can do this!" He will see the frothy-white water, detect the scent of aquatic life, hear the muted mix of gurgle and thunder, and feel a rush as he approaches this challenge. His filters are organized to *notice for* the things that work in life.

Another person paddling his way downriver will see only danger when he notices the rapids up ahead. He will feel tension in his chest and notice that his knuckles are white from gripping the paddle. He will feel his heart race and his breathing change as he thinks, "Holy cow! I'm going to die. What should I do— jump out and swim to shore? I don't know; maybe I can paddle around it to calmer waters. It's not like I'm going over a huge waterfall. That would be much worse. But this is still really dangerous!" This individual's filters are organized to *notice for* what is problematic.

You can begin to understand that the spin people place on events gives them a bias toward either the excitatory or inhibitory form.

The excitatory is a naturally healthier and more potent bias. Successful and influential people like Warren Buffett, Steve Jobs, Bill Gates, Oprah Winfrey, Nelson Mandela, and Barack Obama all make decisions from within a benevolent universe, operating from the excitatory bias. Two perfect slogans that capture the excitatory bias are Winston Churchill's quote, "Success is the ability to go from failure to failure without losing enthusiasm," and, from Dr. Robert Schuller, "Tough times never last, but tough people do."

In contrast, life for those who inhabit a malevolent universe and operate from an inhibitory bias is organized around *noticing for*—and then trying to avoid—limitations. It's the sorting of experiences to find flaws and danger signals. It's "The Evening News" mentality, packaged for easy consumption (*Take in three stories of death and destruction per day . . . with Pepcid*).

Consider a typical scenario where you make a decision from the inhibitory state: Upon being approached by friends to go out dancing one rainy weekend night, you appear exasperated, replying, "You want to do *what?*" Ignoring the smiles and general lightheartedness of those friends, who operate from the excitatory bias, you say, "It's so late! Besides, take a look at the weather. It's raining outside. Do you know how many accidents occur on weekends, with people coming home from clubs and all the drunks on the road—and in the rain, no less?"

Surely you know people like this, don't you? No matter what the situation, they seem to sort for what can go wrong, or what won't work about the idea. At this point, despite having read chapter 1, you might wish to ask, "Why?" "Why do people choose to operate from the inhibitory bias?" "Why do so many of us live within the malevolent universe?" It's not like there's no room for them in the benevolent universe. It's a *universe,* for crying out loud! Space is endless, as are the possibilities there.

DEFAULT: THE "CENTER" OF YOUR UNIVERSE

Do you remember what leads people to make poor decisions? Over time, the external data foisted upon them—the things they are told *should* be true—is in contrast to what is a match and fit for them based on their natural state, their "center," what they most know to be true of them at the deepest level within their bodies at any given moment. In effect, they are out of balance with their true selves when forced to make choices that are not in alignment with their *default* state.

Default is another way of expressing the "generalized desired state," first evident in the body position you hold when you are at your very *best,* a principal component of the Mythogenic Self™ Process developed by Dr. Joseph Riggio. It is derived from the "generative imprint" work of Roye Fraser discussed in an earlier chapter. This is our natural state, which we hold at the deepest level—the one we are born with that represents what is absolutely true of us. Once it manifests in the somatic form (i.e., micromuscular flexions, postural shifts, breathing location—high chest or low abdominal—gestures, and eye movements), it positively affects our beliefs, feelings, and external behaviors that immediately follow.

As stated by Devon White, lead developer of the Human Operating System, "The *default* is the natural state of how you are; when you let go of everything else and what's left is the foundation of your being. It is you at your best, not doing anything. You are born perfectly, as if drop-shipped from the factory with a flawless operating system, just like a brand new computer!"

By "letting go of everything else," White means the behavioral strategies we've adopted to cope with what has been foisted upon us throughout our lives. For example, someone describes you as a child in a certain way—say, cooperative, compliant—and before you even realize it, as an adult, you begin to make choices based on the expectations others hold for you, as well as on what works to get you results, including seeking the approval of others. In such instances, your compliance may have caused you to make decisions using externally based information rather than from your default—the place where choices seem instinctively correct. Such choices may have compromised what you knew to be true in order to decide in favor of what others were telling you *should* be true.

These are people who as children would do anything a parent told them to without questioning why, or requesting some modification of that parent's directive. Years later, they may have become obsequious at work, feeling powerless to suggest a strategy that would deviate from what someone else had suggested, or even feeling powerless to ask for a raise.

As you discovered in the last chapter, the discrepancy between using your *default*—coming from your "center"—and feeling compelled to decide based on what doesn't seem natural (the stuff of *should-be-trues*) can lead to indecision or poor decisions. In the course of moving through childhood and adolescence into adulthood, we encounter a number of trials and tribulations that lead us out of our default state and cause us to effectively generate decisions from the inhibitory bias, inherent in the malevolent universe.

Here's an example that will seem familiar to many of you. Notice the external input and inhibitory state of those involved.

The Dating Game

In recent years, there has been a proliferation of online dating services. The alleged intention behind these online clubs is to help people find love and happiness, but upon further inspection, we can find other agendas afoot.

Online dating services are, after all, businesses. And the primary objective is to stay in business. In that regard, a brilliant strategy embraced and expedited by these dating Web site designers/owners is the creation of a context that operates from the inhibitory bias, the preference of so many people when it comes to making decisions.

This translates into offering prospective buyers choices that include long-term membership for a reduced fee. The presupposition, of course, is that it's going to take you a long time to find the love and happiness you seek, and you will likely make some bad decisions before you make some good ones.

In short, everything from how the sites are structured—the rules and regulations—to the advice from notable people is limited in some fashion and organized from the inhibitory bias. This will seem very normal to those who are accustomed to organizing their decisions around what isn't working in their lives.

Trish B., a corporate executive in a Fortune 500 company in New York City, was advised by three of her girlfriends to join the online dating service to which they belong. The consensus was that, though there are "real jerks" out there, once in a while you come across a man with some potential. The way they put it: "You've got to kiss a lot of frogs before you find your prince." Noteworthy to Trish was the fact that none of her three girlfriends so freely dispensing this advice were currently involved with a man, but they had certainly acquired plenty of warts! Here are some of their comments:

"You want to put in a picture of yourself that makes you appear young. Guys will just delete you if you look older. Oh, and don't wear anything too revealing—just enough to catch their interest."

"Watch out for the guys who go on and on about themselves—how important their jobs are, or how much money they have, or about their possessions. Don't let them con you into a meeting until you find out more about them. E-mail is safe, but don't give out your regular e-mail address. And don't give out your phone number until you are satisfied that they aren't rapists or escaped convicts or something."

"You need to check out whether they are just out for a good time, or if they're really looking to get into a relationship. Watch for players. Oh, and while I'm at it, make sure you find out if they're still married."

"Yeah, and almost as bad is just getting divorced but not yet over the ex. You don't want to get involved with one of those."

"Oh, and one more thing: You need to set a limit on distance. You don't want a guy who lives, say, fifty miles away. I once had a relationship with a guy from Philadelphia. He was nice, but he couldn't meet me after work for a drink or simply come over to my place on short notice—not that I have time for a guy during the week anyway, with my work schedule . . ."

"And find out if he has kids. You have one, Trish, and so do I. You don't want to date a guy that has no kids. Unless they are fathers, they won't have patience with your son. Trust me, I once dated a guy who'd never had kids, and it was a total disaster."

Can you hear the inhibitory bias? So many things to watch out for when making decisions. Imagine, as Trish is sitting there enjoying her drink and chatting with her friends, the effect that this external information (what should be true) is having on her default; all of this external information is pulling her out of that natural state. Can you guess some of the decisions Trish will make as she moves forward and joins this particular online dating site? Here's an excerpt from her profile . . .

I don't want a guy who can't communicate his feelings. I'm not looking for any players! If you're on here just to get laid, keep looking. Another thing—do not expect a response from me without a current picture of you. If you're separated and not divorced, keep looking; if you just got divorced in the past few months, keep looking; if you live outside the city, keep looking. Oh, and I'm allergic to cats, and I don't like dog slobber. If you have a cat or a dog . . .

Then there are those who operate from the excitatory bias, rising above any negativity they may receive from their friends and colleagues, or that they detect from the way the site is structured. Here's an excerpt from another individual's profile . . .

. . . And what most interests me is someone to share life with, someone who can infect me with the smile on his face, someone who can laugh and share all that life has to offer. I enjoy tennis, hiking, antiquing, reading, New York Times crossword puzzles, fine dining, and more. I enjoy life and seek someone who experiences the same. I have two daughters—one going off to college in the fall, the other starting high school. You needn't have children, but experience with them will be a plus . . .

Those who dwell in the benevolent universe make decisions from the excitatory bias. They basically learn to override any negative external data—the bad programming that accumulates from others along the way as they grow up—and instead focus their attention where problems simply are . . . *not!* These are the people who break the chain that tethers them to limitations such as stress, trauma, and other stumbling blocks that can lead to indecision or poor decisions. They embrace the call to arms inherent in President Obama's inaugural address: "Invest in what works!" As such, they lead more potent and resourceful lives, often embarking upon personal adventures that result from decisions they make—decisions that lead to desired outcomes, sometimes in spite of adversity.

RESILIENCE: THE ABILITY TO "AIM HIGH"

Many people possess a quality we call "resilience." These people are more likely to make many more positive decisions based on their default states than from external data. In short, they are able to "bounce back." Merriam-Webster's Dictionary defines *resilience* as "able to withstand or recover quickly from difficult conditions." One interesting example cited in the dictionary is that "fish are *resilient* to most infections."

Speaking of fish, when it comes to making successful decisions in business, Dudley Lynch and Paul Kordis suggest in their book, *Strategy of the Dolphin,* that we act more like dolphins than carps or sharks. Operating from the excitatory bias, the dolphin says, in effect, "I need to leverage current trends and information to create and act on compelling visions." In contrast, carps and sharks, each in their own way, operate from the inhibitory. The carp, for example, acts as if to say "I am helpless, but my suffering has a purpose. Losing comes with life." The shark's behavior reflects the position, "I need to destroy you before you destroy me."

There are many examples of people who, like resilient dolphins, have risen above adversity and poor decisions, leveraging what works in their lives to achieve success in their particular realm. Perhaps you can cite examples from your own life in which you were able to make a series of decisions based on what was possible rather than problematic, holding that positive somatic form to bounce back from challenges or distractions that might have come your way. Can you recall a time when you behaved like a dolphin, rather than as a carp or shark? Similarly, think of people you have known and admired, or those from stories you've read, movies you've seen, and places you have visited who were able to persevere against discouraging odds.

Consider these two very different but noteworthy cases of resilience:

Higher than Hope: Nelson Mandela

Nelson Mandela, born in South Africa, is best known for his lifelong struggle against apartheid, fighting against the inequities inherent in his country's policies. Openly discriminatory acts of exclusion—as well as abuse—were committed against blacks, who represented the predominant majority race-wise in South Africa. Mandela, who was educated and became a qualified lawyer in 1942, joined the African National Congress (ANC) in 1944, and was engaged in resistance against the ruling National Party's apartheid policies after 1948. He went on trial for treason in 1956 and was acquitted in 1961.

After the banning of the ANC in 1960, Nelson Mandela argued for the organization of a military wing, or the *Umkhonto we Sizwe*, within the ANC. His intention was freedom and equality for all citizens of South Africa, and his subsequent decisions supported this goal.

Mandela was arrested for plotting to overthrow the government by violence, along with several of his fellow leaders from the ANC. His statement from the dock received considerable international publicity. On June 12, 1964, eight of the accused, including Mandela, were sentenced to life imprisonment, and he was incarcerated from 1964 to 1990.

During his years in prison, Nelson Mandela's reputation grew steadily. He was widely accepted as the most significant black leader in South Africa, and became a potent symbol of resistance as the anti-apartheid movement gathered strength. Noteworthy in relation to potent decision-making is that, despite having been sentenced to life in prison, he consistently refused to compromise his political position to obtain his freedom, for to have done so would not have been consistent with his *default*. Instead, he continued to make decisions relevant to what seemed a "match and fit" for him while in *default:* creating a multiracial democracy in the country of South Africa.

Nelson Mandela was released on February 11, 1990. After his release, he plunged himself wholeheartedly into his life's work, striving to attain the objectives he and others had set out almost four decades earlier. In 1991, at the first national conference of the ANC held inside South Africa since it had been banned in 1960, Mandela was elected its president. Mandela supported reconciliation and negotiation, and helped lead the transition toward his realized goal: a multiracial democracy, which replaced the apartheid regime of South Africa.

Since the end of apartheid, many have frequently praised Mandela, including former opponents. Mandela has received more than a hundred awards over four decades, most notably the Nobel Peace Price in 1993. Nelson Mandela remains one of the world's most revered statesmen.

The Consummate "Core" Decision-Maker

Steve Jobs, cofounder and current CEO of Apple, has never been a conformist. He is an exemplar of operating from one's "core," or *default*—the way of being that manifests when he is at his best and represents the beliefs, attitudes, and behaviors he most knows to be true for him.

Jobs has made a lasting mark on American consumer culture. Four of his innovations have shaken up the computer, music, and entertainment industries. At the original Apple Computer company, which he cofounded in 1976, Jobs oversaw the design and production of the Apple II, the first mass-market personal computer. Later he developed the Macintosh (best known today as the "Mac"), another in a long list of triumphs. This computer represented a break from industry tradition of the time: It was more aesthetic and user-friendly than his competitors had ever contemplated, much less produced.

A little more than a decade later, Jobs's film production company, Pixar, unveiled the first computer-animated feature film. His most recent blockbuster products, the iPod and iPhone, have now sold many millions of units and have fundamentally changed how we acquire and experience music and a host of other categories of information; as well as how we communicate.

Resilience is an inevitable part of the life of someone who makes so many decisions and holds fast to the goals he sets for himself as he continues to master one achievement after another. Jobs has needed to be resilient because despite his achievements, he has also endured some humiliating failures. His most public fall from grace came at the age of thirty, when he was fired from Apple. His subsequent enterprise—NeXT computers—burned through millions of dollars without ever finding a consistent market for its computer workstations. The sun seemed to be setting on Jobs's future as his shining reputation of being the computer mogul/business genius was beginning to tarnish. During this period in the early 1990s, some speculated that Jobs would forever be known as "the cocky young man who scored an early victory with the Macintosh computer and then never fulfilled his promise."

However, never losing sight of his vision as he continued to make decisions that were a match and fit for him in default, he rebounded. After being forced out at Apple, he bought a special effects company from *Star Wars* creator George Lucas and nurtured it into Pixar, the world's first computer animation studio, which became very successful with films like *The Incredibles, Toy Story,* and *Finding Nemo.*

Jobs's most dramatic vindication, however, came in the last ten years when Apple purchased NeXT and appointed Jobs as interim CEO. Apple was in financial decline and losing a number of its most talented staff members. Jobs restored the company to profitability in just one year—and the "interim" was dropped from his title. He has orchestrated Apple's renaissance with products like the iPod and iPhone.

Two years ago, he was chosen to give the commencement address at Stanford University. He urged graduates "not to waste [time] living someone else's life." Jobs credited his extraordinary track record in part to his allegiance to his inner sensibility, the place from which he made exquisite decisions. "You have to trust in something—your gut, destiny, life, karma, whatever," he said. "This approach has never let me down, and it has made all the difference in my life." Relevant to what you now know about decision-making, in effect, he was summoning the importance of living life from default, and making choices using the criterion of *match and fit* from that way of being.

From large cities to small hamlets, people regularly come face-to-face with their limitations and decide to act resourcefully in spite of them in order to achieve success. This is resilience—the ability to persevere under difficult circumstances and to make elegant decisions from the excitatory bias. These decisions are based on what is possible as opposed to what is limiting, and lead to the achievement of desirable, lasting outcomes. Despite all the trials and tribulations the individuals above encountered, each managed to focus attention where he wanted it most. In short, resilience is about deciding that the benevolent universe is a kinder, gentler place in which to live, and then continuing to make choices that sustain this position—literally, within the body.

A contributing factor to someone's ability to bounce back from adversity may involve unforeseen factors, circumstances that are fortuitous. Malcolm Gladwell, in his latest book, *Outliers,* contends that those who experience success in some endeavor are the products of a steady accumulation of advantages or opportunities that present themselves: when and where you were born, your parents' vocations, the circumstances of your upbringing, and your cultural legacy. In effect, much of what happens to you simply has to do with being in the right place at the right time.

Mandela as a young boy was well grounded in the customs and rituals of his African heritage. The values and attitudes that led him to successfully replace South Africa's policy of apartheid with a multiracial democracy were an outgrowth of the traditions and "royal prerogative" instilled by his parents.

Gladwell also cites another major factor that leads to success: the "10,000-hour rule," where, in the course of pursuing success in a particular area, someone has practiced his craft a minimum of 10,000 hours. This was certainly true for Steve Jobs, who spent years disassembling, rebuilding, and ultimately mastering computers.

Irrespective of fortuitous circumstances, there was a distinct pattern operating in each of the above examples of resilience. In the course of emerging triumphant, these individuals found themselves in both perilous and fortunate situations. Both men made decisions that led to positive outcomes, which led to other decisions, and so forth. The results of these decisions are frequently unknown, but despite this uncertainty, resilient people continue onward with confidence, as if traveling a path—a conveyer belt—toward something that will inevitably occur, but isn't present yet.

One such path that has been dubbed "the pattern of all human experience" is also known as the Hero's Journey. First introduced by the eminent Joseph Campbell in his book, *The Hero with a Thousand Faces,* it will be examined in the next chapter in relation to effective decision-making.

CHAPTER 10

DECISIONS OF A HERO: FOOTPRINTS ON THE PATH TO BECOMING HUMAN

Be yourself—everyone else is already taken.

OSCAR WILDE

The privilege of a lifetime is being who you are.

JOSEPH CAMPBELL

In life there are *patterns,* or ordered sequences of events designed to lead someone toward intended outcomes. Take sewing, for example. A seamstress follows a series of pictorial and written instructions known as a "pattern" that determines the size, shape, and even stitch-type of the finished garment. Football plays consist of *formations* and *sets,* which are patterns of activity designed to lead to a score. Though it appears so sometimes, football players are not just running around on a field, randomly. The patterns that comprise plays bind that seemingly chaotic activity into an ordered form. Basketball is a similar example; players are not simply running in circles, hoping to score. By illustration, Tom Izzo, basketball coach of my alma mater, Michigan State University, has dozens of sets or patterned plays that he runs. Couples run a series of patterns, too, in the ways they interact in their relationships—some useful, some not.

In all of these cases, patterns are really clusters of decisions. In this chapter we will examine a unique pattern of human experience, with examples to illustrate the pattern. You will come to understand how the elements contained within that pattern can facilitate powerful decision-making.

UNIVERSAL MYTHS

So how does someone learn to make good decisions that are effective, useful, and lead to desired outcomes? Certainly, there is a sense in which people have been making good decisions since time immemorial.

Often this sense stems from "transformational" myths that tell the stories of individuals you could call "heroes," and what unfolded in their lives as a result of the decisions they made. These myths describe the essential nature of an individual, where to look to discover it, and how it can be made manifest upon the world.

The late Joseph Campbell, a world-renowned mythologist, said the following about the concepts of *myth* and *mythology: Myth* refers to the *transcendent,* or that which remains beyond the boundaries of the present; *mythology,* then, refers to the telling of the day-to-day stories that contain the *transcendent form.*

The transcendent forms of those individual stories, which are beyond the boundaries of the here and now, are known as *universal myths.* They describe the movement of humanity through time. For example, the universal myth *Success in life requires hard work* is transcendent. You have heard this saying, but so did your father, and, in all likelihood, his father, and so forth. It's beyond the boundaries of the present, as Campbell suggested. Furthermore, the phrase cannot be contained by any one person's story. That is to say, it's not specifically about the series of decisions made by any one individual—it's larger than life.

In practice, *Success in life requires hard work* is inherent in the stories of the musician who practices long hours; the student who puts in weekend time at the library while others are out partying; the first-year law hire—an associate—who spends every waking minute soaking up knowledge in the office, courtroom, and law library; the single mother who holds down a job in addition to raising her children; and the athlete who exercises at a feverish pitch. What these individuals have in common is that the many decisions they've made in service of living out of their mythologies move them along the path of the transcendent, that universal myth with which their stories resonate.

Although the individual may not be conscious of his mythology, it is something that guides his every decision. When a little five-year-old boy plays with his fire truck, he enacts his mythology through the stories he makes up, perhaps about the heroics of rescuing people. In so doing, he is "resonating" with (imitating or attempting to get closer to, through his actions and decisions) a larger universal myth, such as what guides Superman, Batman, Mighty Mouse, Spider Man, and a variety of other superheroes: *Doing good in the world makes me a good person.*

Pertaining to effective decision-making, then, myth and mythology provide a model for how people make choices in a variety of situations; they offer a context in which to base decisions as life choices present themselves.

Campbell was highly influenced by the work of Albert Einstein and Carl Jung, among others. Of great interest to him was the extension of space and time beyond that of any single individual in relation to the choices that individual makes as he moves through various stages of his life. He believed the world could be described and evaluated *whole form*—cumulatively—as opposed to simply mechanistically, as in one decision, one individual, one culture, or one country at a time. Like Jung, Campbell believed there are characteristics—what Jung referred to as "archetypal traits"—that are carried through generations and therefore beyond any one individual. For Campbell, then, this larger, whole-form experience of the world manifested as the aforementioned universal myth. In fact, he decided that there is a larger myth than those held by any one person in the world. From the various cultures and time periods, each with its individual stories or mythologies that contain a vast number of individual decisions, he envisioned a giant myth that takes into account all others subsumed within it—all the people, and all of those individual decisions. To Joseph Campbell, this mega-myth was *the story of becoming human.*

THE HERO'S JOURNEY

In 1949, Joseph Campbell described his formal model of this transformational myth in his book, *The Hero with a Thousand Faces*. He called it the "Hero's Journey." In other words, each of us follows his or her own path with its many decisions on the way to "becoming human." Campbell considered the Hero's Journey to be the prototypical myth of all humans throughout the passage of time, and over the entire planet—developed countries, primitive cultures, and every place in between—as recounted worldwide through the mythological stories he collected and organized.

Specifically, the Hero's Journey is a consistent, sequential pattern of human experience: One thing follows the next, which then unfolds leading to the next, and so on. This pattern is made up of a series of decisions people make as they enter each of the Journey's stages.

By the way, you can't skip a step; that's cheating! In order to move into the next stage, you must successfully make decisions in relation to the events contained in your present stage. By recognizing those stages and understanding how they function, Campbell believed that you experience a sense of movement or "flow" in your life, leading you to make quality decisions that facilitate solving problems, as well as encouraging you to continue along your path to gain new knowledge and insights, which in turn can lead to still better, more refined decisions.

As you progress on this path representing the various stages of the Hero's Journey, facing difficult choices, you achieve wisdom, growth, and independence, and in the process, resonate with the universal myth he referred to as the *journey to becoming human.*

Another way of conceptualizing this is that traveling the path of the Hero's Journey leads you to become the person you most want to be, operating from that internal place where what is most true for you becomes the foundation from which you decide— your *default,* or center. The Hero's Journey, then, is about coming back to form, letting go of all pretense collected over time—all the *should-do*'s from external conditions that frequently led to either indecision or poor decisions—and instead, learning to make better decisions that are a match and fit for you. In effect, it's about having "the experience of *your* life."

Here is an overview of the various stages within the Hero's Journey. They contain the pattern of human experience we all have walked, and continue to walk again and again. A true story about a remarkable woman who may be familiar to you will illustrate each of the various stages. Following this, we will consider some examples of decision-making from within this framework.

The Call

In the beginning, the "hero"—you, for instance—is at rest. Life is somewhat idyllic; things are peaceful. There is comfort in your surroundings, at least in part due to their familiarity. Who by now hasn't heard the expression, "Sooner or later, ya gotta step out of your comfort zone!"

Sometimes life isn't idyllic. There is much unrest and discomfort—even pain. But at least it is a familiar pain, and, after all, this is the comfort zone. Who knows what else is out there? This is where, when feeling so dissatisfied that you decide something needs to change, you will often hear, "Yeah, yeah . . . the grass is always greener." And yet, there is a part of you that wants to decide if it truly is. This is *the Call*. But then, there's another part of you that just can't decide, that remains indecisive about moving out of that comfort zone. This back-and-forth shifting goes on for a time before you actually accept the Call.

There are other times that the Call comes from a sense of curiosity or a thirst for new knowledge and experiences. Ever hear that expression, "A little knowledge is a dangerous thing"? Well, that is sort of what happens in this instance. You begin to get wind of new ideas, new knowledge, what's possible for you out there; what exists, in other words, outside the framework of "you" as you currently know yourself to be.

And so begins the first step on your journey. From being comfortable with yourself and your current state of being (with its attendant decisions, knowledge, and movements within that defined space), you, the hero, are now exposed to that which is beyond what you have ever considered possible—the edge of reality, a change in time and space. The latter idea, influenced by Einstein, refers to the fact that each decision you make, though part of a larger whole (the universal myth), is localized in a particular time and place. Whether or not you decide to accept the Call is, in large measure, a function of where you are.

While sitting comfortably in your living room on a Tuesday evening reading this book, what seems true for you in this moment (regarding a decision you may need to make) is different from that which will occur three days hence, walking through a public, noisy, open-air market, the smell of fresh fruits and vegetables wafting your way as you make selections. At that time, as you continue your stroll, taking in the surroundings and making selections, you might wonder how a choice you made three days earlier could possibly have occurred!

As mentioned, one of those differences in choices that may have occurred to you is whether or not to accept the Call—the call to adventure! You see, this very first step, the Call, invites you into the adventure, offering you the opportunity to face the unknown and gain something of physical, emotional, or spiritual value.

The Call can come in different ways: It can occur as a sudden insight, urging you to change, based on the realization that you feel incomplete in some way and are looking to add another dimension to your life. Or it can come as a transformative crisis, a sudden and often traumatic change in your life—the loss or relocation of your job, the death of a loved one, and so forth. This decision to answer the Call can also be a slow, insidious process—the perennial tease, having been briefly exposed to information that repeatedly presents itself over time as a vague, gnawing sense of discontent, imbalance, or incongruity in your life.

For some, it becomes a matter of restoring honor: their own, their family's, or that of their country. In a related sense, the decision to answer the Call could be about sticking up for the rights of other, more-oppressed people.

So in general, the Call represents separation from the familiar. It becomes an opportunity to make new decisions based on our awareness of a shift in our intellectual, emotional, or spiritual center of gravity. It can happen as a result of discovering that the roles we have heretofore been playing in our society, our environment, are worn thin and no longer fit our needs, and so we decide we should move on to new horizons.

GOING ABOVE AND BEYOND

Amelia Earhart was never content to be the demure female, characteristic of early-twentieth-century women. As a child, she possessed a spirit of adventure characterized by her participation in rough-and-tumble activities usually identified with boys. Fascinated by the roller coaster she saw when on a trip to St. Louis, she became drawn toward the inevitable: flight. This was her Call. As a child, she initially answered it by working with her uncle to cobble together a homemade ramp, fashioned after that roller coaster she'd seen. She secured it to the roof of her family's toolshed, and then, using a wooden box as the car, she fearlessly but foolhardily flew off the roof. Although she sustained some minor injuries, it was worth it for the inexorable sense of exhilaration she experienced!

Her emotional and spiritual sense of gravity had shifted, and she was smitten by the prospect of flight. But as is often the case, the following year at the age of ten, she refused the Call. Amelia had seen her first aircraft at the Iowa State Fair, and one look at the rickety old "flivver" was enough for Amelia, who later described the biplane as "a thing of rusty wire and wood and not at all interesting." However, the Call is persistent; it is a pull toward something inevitable, and her Call would soon emerge again.

Accompanied by a friend, Amelia visited an air fair held in Toronto. One of the highlights of the day was a flying exhibition put on by a World War I ace, Frank Hawks. The pilot overhead spotted Amelia and her friend and dived at them. Amelia characteristically stood her ground, swept by a mixture of fear and exhilaration. As the aircraft came close, something inside her awakened. "I did not understand it at the time," she said, "but I believe that little red airplane said something to me as it swished by." The Call was beckoning again.

Ten years later, she and her father visited an airfield where an aviator, encouraged by her father, gave Amelia a ride. It would forever change her life. "By the time I had got two or three hundred feet off the ground," she said, "I knew I had to fly."

She had answered the Call at last, and would become the most famous woman in aviation history. But first . . .

The Threshold of Adventure

Once we make the decision to answer the Call, we are led by a "guide" (someone or something we trust) to the Threshold of Adventure. This is the jumping-off point, as Campbell referred to it, the interface between that which is known and familiar and that which is unknown.

In the world we know, irrespective of our contentment, we feel secure making decisions because we know the "lay of the land." We are aware of the situations in which we are deciding and the various outcomes that could result from those decisions. Once past the Threshold, however, we enter the unknown, a world containing challenges and dangers, a landscape where deciding can often carry far different consequences than we ever could have imagined!

Often at the Threshold, we encounter people or situations that block or try to discourage our passage across. These are the guardians of the Threshold, and they have two functions: (1) to protect us from taking a journey for which we are unprepared or otherwise reluctant, and (2) to allow us to pass through and make a commitment. That is to say, "I'm ready; I can do this!"

Early on, your parents and teachers functioned as guardians by virtue of the decisions they made for you. By setting restrictions, they tried to keep you safe and prevent those things that could cause harm, even if it meant discouraging you from doing what seemed most natural for you—and most true. At some point, parental guardians make tougher decisions: In measuring our capabilities against the challenges we face growing up, they often push as well as protect in terms of the conditions they impose upon us.

As adults, our threshold guardians are much more insidious and appear in the form of fears and doubts about the possibility of being ineffective and failing.

Amelia's guide to the Threshold was her father. Once she'd committed herself to aviation, following her experience with pilot Frank Hawks, she met her Threshold guardians. Judged harshly by some, beseeched by others to pursue a different path, Amelia made a series of decisions that reflected her determination to learn to fly.

Crossing the Threshold into the unknown to pursue her fascination with aviation, she worked a number of odd jobs, including as a truck driver, to pay for her first flying lesson. To reach Kinner Field, where the lesson took place, she had to take a bus to the end of the line and then walk four miles. She did this not knowing for sure that she would be successful, as female aviators were rare in her day.

After crossing the Threshold, while attempting to navigate the unknown, we often will encounter assistance from others—what Campbell called "magic helpers." Their task is to provide assistance or direction as we make decisions along the way. Often, they bring us a divine gift, such as a talisman, which will help us through the ordeal that lies just ahead. This can occur as "divine inspiration," or a sudden realization about a certain decision.

The most important of these helpers is the one who serves as mentor, keeping us focused on the goal ahead and providing a solid foundation of confidence to help us decide, even under the most adverse of conditions, when the danger is greatest. Having decided to cross the Threshold, these magic helpers serve to build our capacity to move forward in the journey and to continue making more useful decisions as we progress through the stages that follow. After all, we are beginning to gain invaluable experience with each decision made in the unknown, thereby increasing the likelihood of making even better decisions in the future; hence the phrase, "building your capacity."

Initially, Amelia's magic helper was her flight instructor, Neta Snook, a pioneer female aviator. Snook instilled in Amelia the skills and inspiration necessary for flying, which was still in its infancy, and an expression of unrivaled freedom and excitement.

Female aviators were almost unheard of; in fact, in 1923, Earhart became only the sixteenth woman in the world to earn a pilot's license! This was considered as audacious then as female astronauts were in the 1990s.

Continuing to navigate the unknown along her path, Earhart enlisted the assistance of various instructors who helped her perfect her skills. By 1927, she had accumulated nearly 500 hours of solo flying—a very respectable achievement. This in turn led to more decisions, including her association with other fellow aviators, and becoming a member—and eventually the vice president—of the American Aeronautical Society's (AAS) Boston chapter. She also invested a small sum of money in the Dennison Airport and acted as a sales representative for Kinner airplanes in the Boston area. She was building the capacity to function as a knowledgeable aviatrix, who could both fly and sell airplanes and have an impact among her peers in this burgeoning field known as aviation.

The Challenges

At some point, once the Hero crosses the Threshold into the unknown, trials await. These are the challenges that contain increased risk, whether emotional or physical. There may be temptations as well. By meeting the challenges successfully along the way, we build self-confidence, maturity, and the skill set necessary to tackle increasingly more difficult situations along this path. Not atypically, the challenges often strike our most vulnerable selves—our poorest skill, or our weakest spot emotionally. Furthermore, the challenges always reflect the fears we need to conquer so as to turn them from demons into gods; from an evil adversary that can harm you to an ally that can support your best efforts.

Amelia's development as an aviatrix was replete with temptation and risk, and she continued to make decisions along the path of the unknown. With each successful decision in relation to aviation, her confidence grew—and so did her desires. First, her goal was to achieve her license as a female aviator. Then she decided to up the ante and confront another major challenge: She wanted to become the first woman to fly across the Atlantic Ocean, on the heels of Charles Lindbergh.

At first, she decided the challenge was too perilous for her to undertake. Then an experienced pilot asked Earhart if she would like to fly the Atlantic. Although she didn't pilot the plane, she was among the flight crew that made it from Newfoundland to Wales in 1928, and was inspired to tell interviewers, ". . . maybe someday I'll try it alone."

So captivated was she by her trip across the Atlantic that she decided to meet another challenge: her first long solo flight, which occurred just as her name was coming into the national spotlight. By making the trip in August 1928, Earhart became the first woman to fly solo across the North American continent and back. Gradually, her piloting skills and professionalism grew, and she was acknowledged by experienced professional pilots. Through it all, she met another great challenge: gaining public acceptance of aviation, especially in relation to women entering the field.

More challenges, more decisions: Earhart was among the first aviators to promote commercial air travel through the development of a passenger airline service; along with Charles Lindbergh, she represented Transcontinental Air Transport (TAT, which later became TWA), and invested time and money in setting up the first regional shuttle service between New York and Washington, D.C.

The Monsters of the Abyss

This is the cauldron where the hellfire burns bright, where we risk the greatest uncertainty as we conquer the challenges before us. In fact, the obstacles can be so great at this point that we often decide to surrender ourselves completely to the adventure and become one with it. By this, I mean, we completely let go of ideas, decisions, memories of past outcomes, and be fully present in the moment, which allows us the most access to our available resources. We will need all of our strength to "slay the dragon," which often takes the form of something we dread, or simply a formidable task. The risk, of course, is that we may consider ourselves unprepared or in possession of some character flaw, which will defeat us: *The monster will win.* And so here, in the belly of the Hero's Journey, the lowest and yet most crucial point, there is the nagging sense that we may make the wrong decision, and fail.

In 1936, Amelia Earhart confronted the greatest of temptations: She decided to start planning a round-the-world flight, which at 29,000 miles would be the longest flight in history. The flight plan called for her to follow a grueling equatorial route. Three "monsters" confronted her: (1) Weather—could a craft of her time sustain itself through varying and unpredictable conditions that spanned such a vast amount of territory? (2) Endurance—would she be able to stay awake and withstand the relative discomfort for such an extended period of time, even though the trip would consist of three "legs" (places to land)? (3) Technology—would her Lockheed L-10 Electra, a gold-standard aircraft of her day, with specially fitted fuselage fuel tanks, be sufficient to carry her to the various stops along the way? Could she navigate some difficult stretches of terrain—such as the fateful Hawaii to Howland Island portion—accurately?

When she ultimately made the trip, Amelia Earhart and her copilot, Fred Noonan, disappeared somewhere near Howland Island. They were lost at sea, never to be found, despite the intensive search efforts of the U.S. Navy and Coast Guard. But the story doesn't end here.

Transformation and Revelation

Having made the necessary decisions to slay the dragons and meet the challenges within the abyss, we overcome uncertainties—call it *indecision,* for the purposes of this book—and the Transformation is complete. We move from the nagging feelings of incompleteness that lead to the Call—all those times where we decided to not decide in relation to moving forward—to a sense of having acquired new strengths and resources, through a series of successful decisions that were made along the Hero's Journey. In the course of moving from indecisiveness to quality decisions, fear must die so courage can emerge. Having traveled this path, we become enlightened and shed our dependency. We no longer lack the resources necessary to make good decisions; we have a sense of independence and resourcefulness now, and we know how to make quality decisions.

A significant element of the Transformation process is called Revelation. This is a shift in our worldview, moving from deciding as a function of external data imposed upon us to deciding from our *default,* the place from which at the deepest level we know what is most true for us at any given moment.

Having made numerous decisions based on what she knew was most true for her—that she was destined to become an aviator—Amelia Earhart relinquished other choices along the way.

Despite having excelled in science and becoming a nurse's aide, she rejected the opportunity to pursue a career in medicine—or anything else, for that matter; it wasn't who she was. Though she took several odd jobs to fund her flying lessons and related purchases, they were only in service of achieving what seemed most natural to her: flying. There were those who challenged her decision to pursue aviation, citing that as a woman, she would likely fail. But Amelia pressed on, ignoring this external data and excelling in spite of it. This brought her recognition and led to that historic first Atlantic flight. With each subsequent challenge she conquered, she acquired new resources that could be applied to the next set of decisions. These decisions and accomplishments, collectively, transformed her. She had experienced a Revelation.

The Atonement

This is a sort of summary experience in which the Hero, having been transformed, incorporates the changes that occurred from the decisions made on the Journey in order to correct the imbalances or longings that prompted the acceptance of the Call in the first place. We become "at one," or comfortable with our new selves. According to Joseph Campbell, the Transformation "brings us into harmony with life and the world."

Another way of conceptualizing this, consistent with what we have been developing in the last few chapters, is that the Atonement allows us to collectively consider all the decisions we have made on the Journey as an opportunity to move to the center of our being. We then embody what we have learned in the process of resetting to *default*—that peaceful place inside of us, who we most know ourselves to be when we simply let go of the pretense, inherent in all of the external criteria imposed upon us throughout our lives. By operating from *default*, the natural state in which we are born, expressed somatically, we are at peace with ourselves; decisions that emanate from that place will be a function of whether or not they are a match and fit. That is, whether having decided, we can still maintain the position identified as *default*. If so, then life is idyllic once more, and we have reached Atonement.

At the time Amelia Earhart planned her flight to circumnavigate the globe, she had likely assimilated all the positive energy from her previous learning and experience, and from the acclaim she had received as an aviatrix. Judging from the confidence she exuded, she was convinced she could successfully complete this round-the-world flight. What Amelia actually achieved was far greater, as she left quite a legacy. Earhart was a widely known international celebrity during her lifetime. She set aviation records in altitude, speed, and distance flying. Her decision to answer the Call and to pursue a career as an aviatrix transformed her; she became an advocate for women in this growing field, and published two books and scores of articles on aviation. She was in demand and frequently offered lectures. She produced luggage and other products with her familiar AE insignia. There was even a foray into the fashion world, where Amelia promoted a line of women's clothing based on her style preferences: sleek, simple lines made of washable, wrinkle-proof material—ready to take off at a moment's notice!

The Return

Following the assimilation of new learning that occurs during the Atonement phase, we return to our everyday life, bringing home the "gift" that has been bestowed upon us as a result of having made the decisions that led to our new skills and created our new level of awareness. The essence of the return is to share the product of those invaluable decisions—how what we have gained has added to our "being human"—with society.

Amelia Earhart's gift to American women was to raise their self-esteem and encourage them to pursue their dreams. Her charismatic appeal and qualities of independence, persistence, coolness under pressure, and courage led to the achievement of a high-profile career. The message to other women: You, too, can achieve success in something you are passionate about, despite the naysayers!

Amelia Earhart is generally regarded as a feminist icon. Hundreds of articles and scores of books have been written about her life, which is often cited as a motivational tale—*a myth,* as described by Joseph Campbell—especially for girls. Having lived a life true to herself without compromise, Amelia found a measure of peace that many of us seek, and few of us ever find.

The Hero's Journey and Default

A unique aspect of the Hero's Journey is that the decisions made along the way ultimately lead you "home," to a place of acceptance and realization of who you truly are. In other words, the Hero's Journey can be a vehicle of discovery in which wisdom, growth, and independence are achieved, leading you to what Roye Fraser calls the *generative imprint,* mentioned earlier. This is the state in which you are at your absolute "best," first expressed as a position held within the body.

Of paramount importance here is that this place—your *default,* or center—becomes a yardstick against which to determine whether a particular decision is a match and fit for you—whether or not it is truly a good decision. Once again, you will notice how this markedly deviates from perhaps more conventional approaches to decision-making, the emphasis of which is more on the "mind" or how to correct your thinking in the course of making better decisions. It has been my contention throughout this book that the somatic form of those who have decided well differs markedly from that of those who either decide poorly or who are indecisive. Though you obviously cannot observe those people in the illustrations about which you've read, you can certainly learn to become cognizant of your own somatic form. In that regard, you'll find more on how to make good decisions in the final chapter ahead, including how to find and maintain your default.

The path of the Hero's Journey contains many footprints. Here is one more for you to consider.

Magic Fingers

From an early age, Wendy R. knew she had a gift: the ability to bring relief to sore, tight muscles. Her mother thought it was uncanny how Wendy knew where to massage her just from looking at the way she stood, the way she moved. Wendy even brought relief to her twelve-year-old golden retriever, Homer, massaging him for hours. At fifteen, she responded to the Call, and committed to her desire to become a licensed massage therapist.

Wendy was a poor student. For years, her parents had received notes from her teachers, admonishing her for failing to complete assignments, daydreaming during class, and receiving poor grades. In eighth grade, she was classified as learning disabled and carried a second diagnosis of attention deficit disorder (ADD). Rather than her teachers taking notice of the fact that her academic difficulties were a function of information processing, which was largely visually driven and deviated from the preferred auditory channel through which material was presented, they considered her damaged goods and placed her in special education. Needless to say, this did not meet her needs, and she continued to do poorly in school.

At sixteen, by then a high school junior, and after years of negative feedback from teachers and her mother, she decided to refuse the Call, abandoning any hope of attending massage school—or any other post–high school training. Instead, she resigned herself to the possibility that she might not even finish high school. Her mother, sharing that fear, brought her to see me in the spring of junior year, with hopes that I could help her accept her limitations and yet still graduate.

Not accepting the fact that she was damaged in any way, and having elicited her default, through which she expressed her deep desire to be a massage therapist, I became her guide. This of course was first expressed in her body in a particular way that has already been introduced as the somatic form. Keep in mind that accessing a particular position in the body that leads to highly positive, energetic, goal-directed behaviors is something akin to fine tuning a radio to pick up a distant station. Once achieved, however, she learned to make decisions that were most true of her, including applying to a massage school. I had led her to the Threshold. Once across, she would need to make a series of decisions based on what was necessary for her to attend to her studies, graduate, and be accepted at a massage school. Wendy's mother, her major threshold guardian, believed it prudent to offer realistic advice: "Wendy, you're not a student. You don't apply yourself and can't stay focused. I will be very proud of you if you somehow manage to graduate high school and get a job somewhere."

Wendy knew that her mother's advice did not match with her new self-knowledge, so she decided to step across the Threshold into the unknown. She faced many challenges, not the least of which was learning to focus and improve her grades. Wendy began making decisions that sustained her positive way of being: She increased her study time, consistently attended school, and asked her mother to hire a math tutor. Through continued counseling to support her default state, and with the assistance of a "magic helper," her eleventh-grade English teacher—who recognized her visual learning strategy and channeled information accordingly— Wendy raised her grades from barely passing to a C+ average over a three-month period.

It was about this time that she learned of a bridge program: a college-level vehicle that would allow her to leave high school, train for two years in her desired vocation, massage therapy, and through this venue, also obtain a high school diploma. The Challenge was that if she dropped out or failed to complete massage school, she would not graduate from high school. Captivated by this idea, she had reached her personal set of trials, the Monsters of the Abyss. She had to risk it all. If she succeeded, she would both graduate high school and become a massage therapist. Fail, and she'd leave with nothing.

Wendy was frightened. "What if I fail? My parents will have spent this money and I will have nothing. I don't know what to do." Her somatic form had shifted to the inhibitory. It was clear that to slay the monsters, she needed to get past her indecision. Fear needed to die so courage could emerge. I did some more work with her that was "teleologically based" (see chapter 11), and she was able to sustain her default around the choice of having already become a massage thera-pist—just not yet! This would carry her through her studies.

Having overcome her indecision based on fear of failure, she was transformed, encouraged that she could succeed. She had reached the point of Revelation, both understand-ing the external position her parents' advice (to not pursue this course) held for her, and the fact that it was not a match and fit for her in default. Her confidence grew that fall as she began her course of study while continuing to work with me. Each decision she made—what classes to take first term, scheduling study time, arranging for extra help on occasion—reinforced her confidence, first expressed as the position she held in her body, that she had already completed the work necessary to become a massage therapist—just not yet. The more she was able to recognize her somatic form, the easier it was to sustain this potent way of being.

Just before leaving counseling, Wendy reflected upon how consistent her behavior had become. She had achieved the point of Atonement, in which she summarily evaluated her perseverance since junior year regarding all the decisions she'd made about her avocation. She was grateful that she had not succumbed to advice "for her own good," to accept her so-called limitations. In February of her first year of massage school, we terminated counseling.

I've always been an exercise freak, working out a minimum of four times per week. Once, I sustained an injury to my left trapezius muscle, limiting my range of motion, but worse, limiting my workouts. This was unacceptable, so I let my fingers do the walking and found a massage parlor called Magic Fingers. To my surprise and delight, three years after having wished her well, I found Wendy, running her own business! She had returned with her "gift," one that she shared with those in need, including me that day. And I have to tell you, her business was appropriately named.

THE HERO'S JOURNEY AND *YOUR* LIFE

Think of the mythology that guides your decisions, reflected in the stories you tell yourself and others, as well as some of your favorite movies and books that would fit the paradigm of the Hero's Journey.

Go ahead—take a shot at this. Consider how at times in the course of your life, it seems that you've been drawn along an inevitable path toward something you value. Perhaps it's the story of how you selected the college you attended, the job you applied for and landed, the love of your life, your divorce from the love of your life, something you invented or created.

Whatever it is, consider the Hero of your story—you:

1. What was the Call to Adventure that coaxed you out of your comfort zone, into the unfamiliar?

2. Who or what served as your guide, leading you to the Threshold of Adventure?

3. Who were your threshold guardians that may have tried to discourage the Journey by sending you back to that aforementioned comfort zone?

4. What allowed you to pass the guardians and plunge across the Threshold into the unknown?

5. Who were your "magic helpers" or mentors that helped you to make still more decisions as you approached the Challenges, those decisions that could seduce you away from your true path—in other words, bad decisions?

6. What was your experience when you reached the Abyss? What were the monsters or demons that had to be slayed?

7. What was revealed when you were transformed, having made the decisions that led to incorporating important changes into your life?

8. Finally, upon returning home, how did you—the Hero—use this knowledge and experience?

Up to this point, you have been reading a lot about this highly desirable, natural position called *default*. So how do you get there? How do you know you've gotten "there"? It's time to make it happen.

CHAPTER 11

ALL THINGS CONSIDERED . . .

No sensible decision can be made any longer without
taking into account not only the world as it is, but
the world as it will be.

ISAAC ASIMOV

The ability of a person to perform well, to make exquisite decisions, is largely a function of the *framework* that contains those
decisions. And that framework is first evident within your body. It
can be structurally sound or unsound.

Think about your house for a moment: If it is designed of top-
grade materials—fire-retardant Sheetrock, double- or triple-glazed
windows with argon gas between the layers for energy efficiency,
copper wiring that is up to standard electrical codes, brand-new
weather-resistant siding and slate or other quality roofing, and
so forth—decisions that are made in relation to decorating or
appliance upgrading will be compatible with the structure of this
home. In contrast, if the siding on the house is rotting or peeling,
the electrical wiring is of the older aluminum type that may be
more likely catch fire, the roof leaks in places, and the windows
are single-pane, which are not energy-efficient, any decisions that
are made are hampered by these structural limitations. Could you
decide to paint this house before replacing the rotting shingles?
Would a decision to purchase lined curtains, as a way of reducing the draft in the winter from the single-pane windows, really
be energy-efficient? Could you decide to upgrade your kitchen

appliances without addressing the inferior electrical wiring? In a similar way, good personal decisions are made from within a good structure, and that structure is you, at your best.

I have a question for your consideration: "How do you know you're *you*?"

Yes, you read that correctly; but just in case you still think you've misread it, I will state it again: "How do you know you are *you*?"

In reality, this is perhaps the most important question I have posed to you in the entire book. So I will frame it once again, and this time, take a moment to pause and really consider the question, noticing whatever comes up for you. "How do you know you are *you*?"

And no, the answer has nothing to do with what your mother—or anyone else—may have told you. This is a personal knowing from deep within you. It's a place you reference inside, such as right after you get off a cross-trainer or a treadmill, or finish some other form of exercise; or after a good cry, when you have shed all pretense of what someone did to you to make you unhappy, and there's nothing left but *you*; or when you are at your absolute best, becoming present—that is, fully aware of what is around you while shutting down all the noise inside.

In fact, rather than it being about *doing* anything, the answer to "How do you know you are *you*?" is simply about . . . *being*. Just hold this consideration a little while longer, and we will return to the question again later in the chapter.

GATHERING OUR THOUGHTS

So let's reflect for a moment: From everything you have read so far, have you decided whether or not you can move past indecision? Have you given any thought to when and how you *have* made

useful decisions in the past? All things considered, if you have gotten this far in the book, you are well on your way to getting off the
fence of indecision and improving the quality of those decisions
you do make.

Just to be sure we're on the same page, though, let's do a "vita-
min capsule" review; this is a smooth, gelatin-like shell filled with
just enough summary content for you to swallow comfortably
without choking. Ready? Imagine taking one of these capsules
out of a box—call it "Dissolving Indecision." Now, pop it in your
mouth and chase it down with a glass of fresh, cold water. The
ingredients—tiny beads of information from previous chapters
now circulating through your body—consist of the following:

Though you have often asked inefficient questions, such as
"Why can't I decide?", in truth, you have learned how to become
stuck as a result of assimilating a variety of experiences from childhood to adulthood. And you have expressed that indecisiveness or
poor-choice selection first and foremost within your body, held as
an inhibitory position, in which your primary concern has been
the avoidance of problems, all the while believing yourself incapable in those moments of either moving toward pleasure or away
from pain. And now, by shifting your body from the current position that reeks of problems to one that exudes the fragrance of
possibility, you can begin an exciting and challenging journey that
will open doors to wisdom and growth, the products of useful,
satisfying decisions.

The idea of shifting your body into the excitatory bias discussed
in chapter 9, and putting your attention on what is possible—what
works in your life—instead of things that are problematic is syn-
onymous with moving to that place of deep internal satisfaction.
This, of course, is your center, which has also been described as

default: the position you hold when you are at your absolute best. And this is the place from which you can decide, without reservation, based on what is true for you at any given moment. In other words, from this place you can decide as daily choices show up—about play, school, chores, work, relationships, investments, travel, pets, purchases—whether or not a particular choice is a match and fit for you, as opposed to that choice being a demand imposed by another person or institution with a different agenda.

STRUCTURAL WELL-FORMEDNESS

According to Dr. Joseph Riggio, architect and designer of the Mythogenic Self Process, the way we organize ourselves on the inside, irrespective of what is thrown at us from the environment, will determine the quality of decisions we make. As Riggio notes, "Only when a person is internally sound and well-formed will he be able to . . . have the ability to decide and take action, especially in critical situations."

He continues, "A *structurally well-formed* individual is one who is holding a *position* (within his/her body) that reflects who he is at his *best*. This is what occurs when, internally, you are aligned with who you most know yourself to be." That is, you are structurally well-formed when the beliefs to which you adhere reflect an internal posture of you at your *best*, in contrast with a somatic form that is held against choices that are rife with the *should-be-trues* of others.

In short, we are either well-formed or ill-formed, and this has to do with the particular position we hold within our bodies. Being able to function well over time, free of internal conflict, is directly related to how we are structured. This principle holds true for making decisions, which is a way of functioning. To make the choices that are best for us, we need to learn to function in a well-formed manner while holding a well-formed structure.

How Function Relates to Structure

Many individuals learn to become *functionally well-formed,* even though they are structurally ill-formed. The ability to excel at something you are doing, i.e. functional well-formedness, contains two elements: (1) The motivation to produce a specific intended outcome, and (2) the skills to execute in relation to the outcome that is intended.

Having heard that lawyers make a lot of money and knowing that striving to do so was an essential concept in your upbringing, you decide to pursue a career in law. To begin, you may research law schools and start shoring up your undergrad course work in a way that will more easily transition into graduate studies in law school. Perhaps you even request an interview and then visit a law firm. You ultimately apply to law school and are accepted. In this scenario, one would consider you highly motivated to become a lawyer.

Subsequent to that, after having passed the bar exam, if you had been hired by a firm and developed a masterful skill set, say, in the area of criminal litigation or perhaps corporate law, then you will have learned to become functionally well-formed as an attorney.

Structural well-formedness is not about doing anything; it arises from being. Function follows form. When someone engages in a pursuit that is not in alignment with who he knows himself to be—his natural structural form—internal conflict usually results at some point, creating a dilemma reflected in having difficulty making decisions. This is why it is crucial for you to understand the difference between structure and function as these are applied here.

The Natural Structural Form Applied

Someone's *natural structural form* is that position held within the body that has heretofore also been described as one's center (*default*). Recall that this is the place you go within your body that is aligned with or matches what you believe is true for you at the deepest level at any given moment. In this position, whatever comes up will either be a match and fit for you in this form, or it won't be, in which case you will experience a shift in the way you are holding this choice—literally. In other words, when a choice is not a match and fit for you in *default,* your body will assume a different somatic form—in all likelihood, a compromised, inhibitory form around the information being considered, which will seem unnatural (the stuff of should-be-trues).

In the previous example, a lawyer is structurally ill-formed if who he most knows himself to be at the deepest level is not in alignment with the decisions he has made in the field in which he is functioning. That is to say, somatically (at the deepest level within his body), perhaps who he most knows himself to be—his natural structural form—is a highly creative individual who embraces music, architecture, or psychology—but not law. And when he needed to make decisions related to pursuing law, when his body was clearly in *default,* he decided to forego them in deference to what others taught him *should be true*—that he should pursue a legal career.

Under the circumstances, it could very well become difficult for him to continue making useful decisions in relation to his ongoing position as an attorney. This is the type of individual who sometimes becomes increasingly more disenchanted with the work in which he is involved and starts reevaluating his life later on, often the stuff of a midlife crisis. In contrast, here's another example.

Structure and Function in Sync

Recall chapter 9 in regard to the concept of resiliency, and the example set by Nelson Mandela. He was South Africa's best-known and most beloved hero, jailed numerous times for causes he believed in surrounding the elimination of apartheid and other political injustices. In effect, he sacrificed his private life and his youth for his people, never wavering in his devotion to democracy, equality, and learning.

Think of the many decisions Mandela had to make during these trying times. Despite terrible provocation, he never answered racism with racism. His life has been an inspiration, in South Africa and throughout the world, to all who are oppressed and deprived of civil liberties. He held fast to what he knew to be most true for him, rather than succumbing to what others told him should be true.

The point is that although he was oppressed, and his jailers tempted him numerous times by offering to commute his jail sentence in exchange for giving up his position, he neither changed that position nor built up the kinds of emotional resentment that would cause him to make bad decisions. He did not become a terrorist or a rampaging killer, as Idi Amin did. Instead, holding the position within himself that best represented who he knew himself to be, he became a statesman and was able to espouse the principles to which he had dedicated his life. He remained structurally well-formed and could then function as president of the ANC in a functionally well-formed manner.

IDENTIFYING STRUCTURAL WELL-FORMEDNESS

So how do we express structural well-formedness? We begin by accessing our most positive experiences, usually through stories that we tell others and ourselves that reveal our fascinations and talents. These experiences first occur to us as a position held within the body, the *somatic form*. The form we hold in our bodies as we consider our very positive experiences then becomes the lens that focuses us toward gradual awareness of what is possible when we are simply *being*, holding a well-formed position. The outcome? When holding this powerful position that represents who we are at our very best, we can make more self-enhancing decisions. It's about how our performance results from this internal stature, and, *like this*, how we can make decisions that will lead to positive effects on our health and well-being.

There is another way to access the position you hold when you are structurally well-formed. Look in a mirror and ask yourself the question introduced previously: "How do you know you are *you*?" This is the ultimate of decisions. It represents your original blueprint—how you were designed. You will see this question again and again. Although you may not master it right away, begin to pay attention to where you go inside to retrieve the answer. You will need to train yourself to notice tiny details. It's a position—the path your eyes take to retrieve different kinds of information; it's any postural shifting, perhaps a head tilt, different muscle flexions, or breathing changes. Play with it! We will return to it with some specific suggestions again later in the chapter.

STRUCTURAL ILL-FORMEDNESS

By way of comparison to Nelson Mandela, who was an exemplary case of structural well-formedness, consider Michael Jackson for a moment. He represents the antithesis: structural ill-formedness. Noteworthy was the song he composed, "Childhood," a classic in which he sings, "Have you seen my childhood?" And a few bars later, "It's been my fate to compensate for the child . . . I've never known." And he didn't.

Michael Jackson had a rare talent that catapulted him to fame at the age of five. His performances captured audiences young and old. He was an iconic star from his earliest beginnings, banging the bongo and performing with his brothers as the Jackson Five, and then later achieving his many milestones in the entertainment world.

Because he performed as a young child, he never really had much of a chance to be one. His father, Joseph, set a strict, regimented schedule for Michael and his brothers. Relentless hours of practice left very little time to do normal kid activities. The decisions Michael Jackson made were imposed upon him through the external input of his father, his agent, and others in the collage of people that directed Jackson's show business career. As he frequently had to subjugate what he knew was true for him at the deepest level and choose what should be true, he was structurally ill-formed. Despite his way of being, he could function extremely well; in other words, he was *functionally* well-formed—at least, for a while.

But although someone can function in a well-formed manner, meaning the actions in which he engages produce the outcomes intended, it is difficult to maintain this over time due to the mounting discontent and the subjugation of decisions that most represent who you are in service of satisfying other "masters."

Michael experienced much disenchantment within himself, exemplified by the drive to constantly change who he was. He surgically altered his facial features. He lightened his skin. He wore that white, sequined glove much of the time, as well as dark sunglasses; and he abused painkillers and other drugs. In the end, trying to remain functionally well-formed while perched on an ill-formed foundation, his *being* collapsed like a house of cards.

It's important to remember that massive dissatisfaction, disillusionment, and indecision often result from an enormous disparity experienced from having made choices over many years that go against what seemed natural and true for you, in order to satisfy the directives of others (all the *should-be-trues*). This disparity is evident across the institutions of our society—family, education, industry, law, and religion, to name a few. We live in a complex society, and the hand we are dealt—the choices available to us from our environment—in many ways directly determine our fate. Lots of rules and regulations; lots of people making sure we follow them; and lots of times when what we are told should be true doesn't seem true, and yet, as those things are often acknowledged and rewarded by society, we bypass our internal experience and do those things anyway, again and again. Ultimately, over time, this leads to the aforementioned indecision and poor decisions. Michael Jackson often chose poorly, and it eventually cost him his life.

Now, where does all this information that may be divergent with what seems true for a particular person come from? What gives rise to all of that external input that is imparted throughout our development, about which we often need to make decisions?

DECISIONS AND "INSTITUTIONAL FORMS"

Interestingly, indecisiveness and poor decisions are virtually absent among aboriginal societies. In all likelihood, people raised in such cultures realize from early on that the life they are living is a match and fit for their internal default experience. Decisions are obvious for them. This is because in their culture, the situations that exist for them are naturally organized and align well with their environment. There is no need to be indecisive. When you are out hunting and a particular animal appears, you strike. When you are looking for a certain medicinal plant, you select it and put it in your satchel. When the children reach an age appropriate for procreation, they select a mate and get on with it. When did you last read about a primitive tribe suffering from an identity crisis?

By comparison, according to Oxford scholar Dr. John Searle, professor of philosophy at the University of California, Berkeley, we live within a paradigm of arbitrary rules and strictures he calls *institutional forms*. We have made up a series of guidelines for how to live our lives based on what we decide is right or wrong. Too often, these guidelines are not grounded in scientific or other sound evidence, and yet we make people decide based on these edicts of right or wrong. Aboriginal societies lack these institutional forms, and so their decisions often make much more sense to them; that is, they are more aligned with what they know to be true for them at the deepest level.

As an illustration of institutional forms, for many years one of the rules and strictures of civilized European society was a prohibition against interracial, interethnic, and interreligious marriage.

It was simply wrong to do this, and everyone within this time and space knew it was wrong. And yet, there were occasions in which two people would meet and for whatever reason, there was an attraction. Their bodies were saying, "This isn't wrong. In fact, this is very, very right!"

Think, for example, of Shakespeare's *Romeo and Juliet.* These young lovers knew at their deepest level, based on what was true for them, that they should be together. But the cost of such compelling desire was that they both perished; they made the ultimate sacrifice to honor a choice they couldn't make because society forbade it. Their unfortunate demise was the ultimate expression of indecision.

Searle's point is that we create these institutional forms that are, in fact, based on language; they really don't exist apart from the value we assign to them (for example, "marriage"), compared with a description of something that already exists in nature (a "mountain"). Then we make up rules and strictures in which we teach people how they need to decide in relation to any one of these forms.

Recall from an earlier chapter the rigidity and limitations we impose on those we raise, educate, or supervise when we adopt the Aristotelian principle of *this or that.* You can do one thing or the other, but certainly not both. This is another illustration of Searle's concept of institutional forms. In contrast, by becoming more flexible as a society and opening up the possibilities that exist in a *this-and-*that paradigm, we include a wide range of choices, which increases the possibility that a decision will be consistent with someone's internal experience—and that a person will have the opportunity to select from among many choices based on what is most true for him in that moment.

As an example of Searle's point regarding two people living together, "marriage" is a contract or institutional form created to sanctify or validate the feelings that two people already have for one another by virtue of the fact that they are living together, a decision they made based on what was most true for them in a particular moment. But in some avenues of society, we castigate them if they are living together outside the institutional form of marriage. In other words, we tell them to decide in relation to the values we offer them—what should be true. Did you get the "this *or* that"? You can either live together married, or remain unmarried, but not living together.

A similar example of institutional forms in which contrived, should-be-trues are imposed upon the behavior of others is inherent in the issue of gay marriage. There are many other such forms within our society.

Then there is education. If you don't pass this tenth-grade math test, you won't succeed in life; you are putting your entire future at risk because your future is based upon your being able to prove that you test well. And in order to test well, you have to do this work. Again, this *or* that; get it?

Now open the lens to include this *and* that. Though you may not get into college with your current study habits or grades, there are many examples of people who have made other decisions that did not include going to college and who nevertheless became enormously successful. Particularly within the commercial domain, think Richard Branson, Bill Gates, and Michael Dell—all of whom made other choices.

REJECTING INSTITUTIONAL FORMS AND DECISIONS

So, making a good decision often has to do with rejecting the fundamental learning that you have been taught—those external inputs of should-be-true—as being the *absolute truth*, indicative of a this *or* that paradigm. Instead, in order to make a good decision, it becomes important first to access your center, and then operating from a this-and-that paradigm, take the opportunity to determine if a particular choice is a match and fit for you when holding this position.

To illustrate, given the choice to select a partner of the opposite sex, in which I am embracing heterosexuality, or a partner of the same sex, a homosexual choice, can I choose heterosexuality as being consistent with what seems a match and fit for me in default while still holding present the fact that I respect someone else who makes the other choice? (Notice the "this *and* that" here.) Can I decide that college seems a match and fit for me, but also recognize and accept that it may not be a choice for someone else? And furthermore, can I decide to respect a certain individual for his choice, despite having been told by him, "If you don't get good grades in high school and get into college, you won't succeed in life"? When you operate from a this-and-that paradigm, the answer to all of these questions becomes an emphatic, "Yes!"

YOU, AS THE CENTER OF YOUR UNIVERSE

The task, then, is to reset to your default position. As various situations occur, it becomes important to sustain that position of default for extended periods of time in order to decide if any particular choice is a match and fit for you.

Now, much as an individual can adopt an inhibitory somatic form (which reflects his constant immersion in the things that can go wrong), or an excitatory form (in which his attention is directed to what is possible in life), society as a whole can embrace one of these two modalities as well. What this amounts to on a cultural scale is living in a benevolent or malevolent universe, depending on a particular society's "posture."

To the extent that we as a society can shift the frame of reference from what could be a problem to what becomes possible by embracing a this-*and*-that paradigm, it becomes much more comfortable—and more likely—for someone to make a positive, useful decision that is aligned with his default position. This was perhaps the most salient outcome of the Hero's Journey from the last chapter: coming home, or returning to form (default).

We began here with a question posed to you. Now, perhaps, you will have one: "So, is there a way just to 'go there'—to reset to default? And if so, how do I do that?"

You want to know how to get to your center, where you can decide from a posture that reflects being true to yourself—where you are at your best—rather than being forced to decide based on the externally imposed choices of society? You might also add, "Once I do, how do I know I *am* 'there'?"

I will respond to both questions by posing mine again: *How do you know you are you?* Pause and hold this consideration a few seconds longer this time. Then let's continue . . .

HOW YOU BECOME *YOU*

Let's take first things first. According to Roye Fraser's generative imprint, way back when you were just a little tyke, something amazing happened for the first time that was a really positive experience for you. I mean a real eye-opener—something that totally absorbed your attention and gave you pause. I also refer to this as "aesthetic arrest," meaning an experience that has totally absorbed all of your senses—visual, auditory, and kinesthetic. It's like a total "Wow!" all over your body. You have many aesthetically arresting experiences as adults (consider art, music, and nature—something that utterly captivates you).

Returning to that earlier time, you would have been completely mesmerized by whatever was going on; you would have been in a positive and resourceful frame of mind, and you would have felt settled within yourself.

Now keep something in mind here: A powerful way in which we learn, develop, and grow is by imprinting experiences into the very core of who we are. These "imprints" occur first and foremost, remember, as positions held within our bodies (somatic form). A particular somatic form—in this case, a very positive, natural one—remains available to us for the rest of our lives.

This means that those positive emotional experiences, which were imprinted in you, represent you at your best. And the mood—the mind-set—of them will return whenever you adjust your body to that particular somatic form you hold that reflects those imprints. Think of it like fine-tuning a radio—you have to slowly turn that knob to get the perfect setting for the best clarity of sound.

"Oh, so holding this position within my body of being at my best means I will be deciding stuff based on my internal criteria rather than someone else's? And this will lead me to make better decisions?"

Yes, on both counts.

"Cool. So how do I get there, already?"

By now, you are likely already there.

How You Can "Get There"

As Joseph Riggio has noted:

> [The task is] to find the original position you held, which defines
> who you are, and stand resolutely in that position despite all
> evidence to the contrary, at all times . . . [Doing this] is about
> reestablishing contact with your original way of being, literally
> being who you are essentially, in the most primal way—going to
> your core and starting there.

Think of a time when you needed to be extremely creative or
resourceful. Maybe it was a business transaction you were able to
craft at work, or a time when you successfully convinced someone
to make a good decision. Think of one of your fascinations, passions,
or greatest achievements—things you know to be extremely pleasing
in some way. Perhaps you are captivated by sunsets, or the won-
ders of nature early in the morning as you stroll through your yard.
Maybe it's a particular genre of movie—love stories, or sidesplitting
comedies. Or it could be a type of art, like sculpture, or architecture.
Take your time to consider these things and simply pay attention to
what comes up for you, especially within your body.

An Unsuspecting Talent

Many of you will recall the international myth that emerged literally
overnight in 2009, called Susan Boyle. Appearing on the TV show
Britain's Got Talent, Boyle stated that it had been her lifelong dream
to be a singer, but that no one had ever given her the chance before.
She was chasing her dream of being as successful as Elaine Paige, star
of British musical theater. At her mother's behest, she pressed on and

ultimately appeared on the show. Notice how this would plug into the template of the Hero's Journey. At the point we first see her, she has crossed over the Threshold and is confronting her demons—her lack of confidence. To "come home again," fulfilling her dream with confidence, she needed to slay the dragon, which translated into impressing the three judges: Piers Morgan, Amanda Holden, and that pompous ass (which may or may not be the branding he exudes rather than a true personality flaw), Simon Cowell.

Boyle began to sing "I Dreamed a Dream" from *Les Miserables*, and within the first eight seconds of the song, there was a noticeable shift in Simon's body. His jaw dropped, his eyebrows lifted, his breathing shifted to further down within his abdomen as he leaned forward, elbows on the table, his chin cradled in his hands. A smile came over his face. The other two judges' eyes welled with tears and they seemed to have lumps in their throats the size of grapefruits from the way they swallowed. Smiles came across each of their faces as well. Their bodies had stilled. All the initial flippant gestures that were apparent when Boyle first emerged on stage had stopped. The shift in their bodies and on their faces seemed totally ingenuous and very pronounced.

As the song progressed and Susan hit every note, Simon's expressions seemed out of character for him. He was glued to this woman in a way that seemed as if he were willing her to succeed. My contention is that all three judges had shifted to the excitatory bias, in which they were at their best. They had achieved a state of aesthetic arrest! Rather than noticing for problems, their trademark behavior as critics on this show, they were *noticing for* possibility. They had reset themselves to default, from which they overwhelmingly decided in Susan Boyle's favor.

RETURNING TO FORM

So once again, "How do you know you are *you?*"

Perhaps now it is clear that in order to answer that question, your body shifts to that natural place for you, which is your generative imprint; it's you at your best, or default. Pay exquisite attention to this. Do it repeatedly, while sitting in front of a full-length mirror. Share this experience with a friend or family member and ask that person to study the changes in your body when you ask the question aloud. As most people are unaccustomed to noticing somatic changes—even eye movements—you will likely have to do this several times in order to get feedback.

Many people who discover this sense of who they are at their best report a number of bodily sensations. Some of these include: a place inside, of silence or "letting go," often located in the thoracic region (your torso, basically), as small as a pinpoint or as large as a coin; a subtle head shift or neck realignment, with changes to the musculature associated in and around the upper neck, where the skull attaches to it; a flexing of the muscles in the lumbar region (lower back), causing an elongation of the spine, a sensation of being taller; a lowering of the shoulders as those muscles relax; a change in both the rate and location of breathing—fast to slower, and either from lower in the abdomen or higher in the chest; changes in temperature and sensations such as a cooling or warming, accompanied at times by chills or tingles; changes in facial muscles; and movements of the eyes either upward or downward, and also to the sides.

Keep in mind that these are unique to each individual and very, very subtle changes—subtle, like watching the hands of a clock move! So if you are expecting a number of gross motor movements, you will miss the subtlety of what is going on. Practice becoming aware in the moment of what you "do" when you are being you, in default, and you will become accustomed to recognizing yourself in that state—one of being structurally well-formed.

Ever watch professional golf? Notice that there is a structural form—an alignment—that when held leads to hitting shots that go where you predict they should, as opposed to someplace they should not. Function, you may recall, always follows form. Holding a well-formed structure in relation to golf, your swing will seem effortless, and even the ball will have a certain sound to it that connotes success.

Similarly, once you master your default position, you will become more skilled at making decisions that are most aligned with who you are (when you are holding this internal state). The result is that your decision-making "swing" will seem effortless, and you will become more successful at connecting your actions to your intended outcomes. The actions you take as a result of your decisions will generate what you expect to happen, instead of something you haven't counted on. Because whatever those actions are, based on the decisions you make going forward, they will represent what is a match and fit for you in the moment you decided, rather than representing the voices of others who demand that you choose what they think should be true, which, as you know by now, can lead to a good deal of life dissatisfaction as these discrepancies accumulate over time.

If the Shoe Doesn't Fit

Here is a typical scenario to illustrate these points. A woman purchasing a pair of shoes will typically try on many before deciding. You may ask, "Why can't she decide?"

Let's take a closer look. The salesman, whose primary objective, of course, is to make the sale, will likely encourage her as she tries on each and every pair.

"Ooh, those look wonderful—go check them out in the mirror."

"This color is really you!"

"The sleekness of those will draw all eyes to your legs."

So then, how does this external information she is receiving about her decision to purchase, biased by the salesman, compare with the signals she is getting from inside herself? One possibility, in relation to any particular pair of shoes she has tried on, is that, when holding default, the idea of purchasing that pair comes up as not being a match and fit: A big, "No!" Perhaps her body registered that these shoes are tight across the instep and the very stylish toe design allows very little breathing room. But then, who needs toes to breathe, right? And the heel is slipping, her foot slightly stepping out of the shoe with each footfall, causing some balancing difficulties. But she is momentarily indecisive. Why? Because on the one hand, the salesman, the guy with the dollar signs in his eyes who is fawning all over her, has his agenda; her boyfriend, who accompanied her to the store for moral support (but wants to get home to watch a football game) has his own; and two other ladies present who are waiting for help from that same salesman (and offered her a few spurious compliments) have their own motive (they want to get out of there sometime today!). All of this, while on the other hand, her internal experience is screaming at her that none of these shoes are a match and fit—and especially not a fit!

Should she make the purchase, she would be acquiescing to the external position of what should be true, according to all the people present, in spite of what her internal experience is telling her is true. This, of course, would render it a poor decision, all things considered. If, however, she politely gets up, takes her boy-friend's hand, and says, "Let's go," she would have decided from a structurally well-formed position, what was most true for her in this instance, resulting in a decision that was highly beneficial. (Later that night, her feet would thank her!)

THE FUTURE INFORMS THE PRESENT

There is one more vital element in the mix, in my professional opinion, the absence of which greatly contributes to "Why can't I decide?" But its presence most definitely contributes to the making of highly significant decisions in life. This is the element of *teleology*: the future, or what is not yet present. This is the bringing into being, through the decisions we make, ideas that can only be held initially as a vision or a dream. Yet, in deciding "teleologically," the events under consideration are held as having happened already—just not yet. This type of deciding takes into account a wider range of consequences—those that will have a huge impact on other people and events—than does simply deciding based on the outcomes of previous decisions, or those that only affect this moment.

In regard to teleology, Dr. Riggio states,

> It's about both giving up your past, or at least your miscon-ceptions and misperceptions about it, and simultaneously acknowledging and accepting it all, without judgment; and then just letting it all go again. Then it's about looking

forward—projecting yourself into your future—stepping fully into your own becoming.

Teleological decisions are like magnets, creating a "pull" forward from your future, unlike so many decisions that are historically based, in which you feel like you are being pushed from your past. Riggio continues:

Most people live historically, dumping their unsuccessful pasts (rife with poor decisions) in front of themselves. In effect, they allow their history to determine their future, limiting themselves by the stories they tell themselves and others about where they've been, and what they've decided or were unable to decide. Deciding teleologically is about recognizing what you haven't done— yet, what's out there in front of you waiting to be done. Fulfilling the yearning of becoming what you are capable of being, fully and magnificently.

All things considered, how many times have you decided something based on worst-case scenarios, or "away from" motivation strategies? These choices have their roots in past performances gone badly, in all likelihood.

Decisions are so frequently tethered to the past that this link seems invisible—yet it is all too present. Do you ever pay homage to past fears by deciding in favor of avoiding something you might otherwise never hesitate to do? Do you decide to refrain from asking for that raise, a date, a discount, or other preferences, citing your having been raised by a stern father who disdained a child speaking out of turn or voicing an opinion? Are you reluctant to pursue a particular course of action because you believe you will probably fail—again? This could be anything from making a purchase or volunteering to head a project at work, to getting married a second time. When you decide what to do going forward based on what has not worked before, any decision you do make will always be in relation to that limitation. You will wear it like an albatross around your neck, weighing down your decisions.

In chapter 9, recall the story, "The Dating Game." Having this additional perspective in looking back, you can see how Trish B. had become a victim of her own decision-making process. Given the advice of her well-meaning girlfriends, experienced online daters themselves, each move she made was predicated upon taking precautions to avoid something that *could* go wrong. In the process of offering allegedly sagacious advice not uncommon to this area, these women were projecting their own unsuccessful pasts onto their girlfriend, Trish. The rule they were operating by was that the future is determined by avoiding the pitfalls of the past.

This historically based paradigm for making decisions is common to all walks of life—work, relationships, family, purchases, and vacations; it even applies to renting a movie. I once overheard a woman in a video store offering enlightenment to another customer regarding the rental of a movie that starred a particular actor. Keeping his name anonymous, this woman stated something on the order of, "Ugh! I wouldn't see another movie with [so and so] in it. I saw the one he made last year, and it totally bombed. His language could use some mouthwash, too. Every other word was the F-word." As it turned out, the movie she was referring to had starred this individual as an escaped convict. It actually did quite well in the box office. In the newer movie, the one the customer was holding as she listened to this litany of unsolicited advice, this individual played a single father in a comedy—two totally different genres! The woman who was giving advice clearly made historically based decisions.

The great advantage of deciding "from the future" is that what has limited you in the past is not necessarily present there. You get to decide what to place in your future without the limitations of the past, and the decisions you made from an inhibitory bias. Instead, you choose with intentionality the outcomes you most want. But the best part is that rather than experiencing a sense of constant pushing from the hands and voices of others, demanding that you become who they need you to be to fulfill their expectations of you, you get to choose freely, becoming exactly who you want to become, stepping effortlessly forward and assuming the default position to produce the outcomes that are the best match and fit for you. Now, how great is that?

What is the impact of decisions in which the future seems to inform the present? Consider, for example, that approximately 200 years ago, the idea of people being able to communicate with someone thousands of miles across the globe in real time by voice, or by voice with visual capabilities thrown in, through a box containing a screen that emits light—well, this was unthinkable. And yet today, it is a concept that is nearly as prevalent as a microwave oven for those of us in the Western world.

Two hundred years from now, ideas, conventions, and technology will spawn new creations, from decisions that are based on what can occur when we are pulled toward a future that contains nothing but possibilities.

FOR YOUR CONSIDERATION . . .

How do you make decisions that are teleologically based? Here are a few suggestions:

1. Make sure you begin from *default*. By now you realize that each of us has his or her own way of getting there. Remember, this is a body position you hold that represents your internal state when you are structurally well-formed, at your best. The advantage of deciding from this place is that things will either be a match and fit for you here, or they will not, and you will decide accordingly.

2. Since teleological decisions begin as a future consideration, you want to ask yourself, "How will I know when I already have [whatever you happen to be deciding]?" Again, pay attention, somatically. How will your body represent this thing or event already having happened? Imagine for a moment that you have just won a trip someplace, or that your boss gave you a raise yesterday. You decide the car you keep passing in the showroom window on your way to work is finally affordable. Tomorrow you plan to bring home a new puppy for your children. And if you're single, maybe the day after tomorrow, someone you love will have said, "Yes!" Step into one or more of these experiences, or something similar of your own choosing, and notice what happens within your body.

3. What will be the impact of your future-based decision on others within your circle of influence? Consider the

people that will show up once you have decided, and
how your decision will affect each of them. A number
of people believe all decisions are "transpersonal,"
meaning, they involve consideration of other people
and things within the system that go beyond just you.
Some notable examples include John Clippinger,
who wrote *A Crowd of One*. He views our identity as
inexorably tied to our relationships with others. Dr.
Daniel Siegel posits that interpersonal experiences,
such as perceiving and responding to social situations,
shape brain development. And Dr. Clare Graves developed
a theory of how cultures evolve through time as a function
of social interaction, which causes shifts in the values we
embrace, as well as increasing the potential brainpower
available to all of us.

A common theme here is that making decisions is always
about more than just you! And having the wisdom to utilize this
idea to your advantage can lead to making some highly exquisite
decisions.

A Living Legend

In considering teleological decision-making, I am reminded of a
miraculous story that occurred early in 2009, in which an ordinary
person—who happened to be an experienced pilot affectionately
known as "Sully" Sullenberger—successfully landed a jet aircraft
with 155 people aboard in the Hudson River. How many of you
watched the news stories about this hero? How did you feel when
you heard this story? Recall the details: While in ascent from
LaGuardia Airport, he encountered some birds that were sucked

into the engines, causing them to fail. The pilot then had a series of decisions to make: lifesaving decisions.

How do you suppose he filtered information? Do you think his decisions were historically based? For example, do you think his attention was focused on other times he might have witnessed or read about in which a pilot faced perilous events that cost him dearly? When those birds hit the engines, do you think Sully went, "Oh my G-d! We're all gonna die—this is terrible"? I mean, imagine him running a lot of inhibitory garbage in his head, like, "Just my luck—those damn birds! They had to be right there—couldn't wait a few seconds more till after we passed through ten thousand feet!" Of course he didn't do that.

I contend that at the time of this fortuitous incident, Sullenberger had already experienced the events that would unfold—whole cloth—just, not yet.

Evidence that his decision-making was future-based came from the *Late Show with David Letterman*, on which he appeared several weeks after this heroic feat. Letterman asked him, "Sully, tell me—what was it like knowing that there was no way to know for sure what was going to happen?" To which Sullenberger replied, "On the contrary—I was aware of what was going to happen. [His body shifted, noticeably.] First, I was just trying to rule out an alternative place to land. When Teterboro was determined to be too far, I knew exactly what would come next. We were going into the Hudson. All I had to do was keep the wings level and the nose up. I had been training for this day my entire career, and had everything mapped out in my mind." This was exquisite. He knew just what he had to do based on having played out that experience in his head—many times! Although I would add, without his fully realizing it, he had generated that experience throughout his body and expressed it as such when he suddenly needed to spring into action.

In contrast, here's a story I used to use when teaching some psych classes regarding decision-making. On the surface, it's about an airplane, but in reality, it's about much, much more.

Airplane Crash Story

Tower: This is the tower calling the captain of flight #6704. Come in, please.

Captain: This is the captain of flight #6704; what do you want?

Tower: Your course is erratic. We are having difficulty tracking you on our radar. Please give us your instrument readings.

Captain: Look, I'm too busy flying this plane with over 165 passengers to waste time looking at instruments.

Tower: But you seem to be encountering turbulence—how is the craft holding up?

Captain: Holding up? What do you expect from a piece of junk like this. It's falling apart. I've asked for new wings, but my requisitions just get ignored. If it doesn't fly properly, it's not my fault. And another thing—why don't I have a third officer in this cabin? It isn't fair. I know a lot of pilots on other airlines that have it much easier. I can't control this plane with insufficient help.

Tower: How about the flight attendants? Perhaps they can help.

Captain: Don't be absurd. I can't count on them. They don't care about my problems. They're always catering to someone else. When it comes to the difficult work, I always get stuck with it. This isn't exactly a 767, you know!

Tower: Captain, the turbulence is increasing. Are your passengers all right?

Captain: Are you kidding? Every flight, I get the worst group. Why, you should just see them—I wouldn't be surprised if they tangled up their oxygen masks and put on their life jackets inside out! What am I supposed to do when I'm working at such a disadvantage? What do you EXPECT?

Tower: Crash!

You probably would not choose to be a passenger on a plane operated by this pilot. Interestingly, a number of people have voiced their desire to be on a plane flown by Sully Sullenberger. In fact, on October 1, 2009, Sully flew a completely booked aircraft from North Carolina to New York and back. On the surface, it seems like he did something extraordinary. But ask him, and he will tell you he was simply being Sully, a man living life at his best—from *default*—such that doing whatever came up in a particular moment was an illustration of his structurally well-formed being in action!

SO, ALL THINGS CONSIDERED . . .

It has been my intention to offer you some new choices in an effort to move you off the fence and give you the opportunity to decide, exquisitely. In that spirit, I wish you the life of your dreams, one in which you are deciding from a position of intentionality—living your life on purpose! And a purpose that is truly your own, based on it being a match and fit for the internal state you are holding—the one that answers the question, *How do you know you are you?*

In the words of Dr. Joseph Campbell, "Follow your bliss." I assure you, having written this book, I am truly following mine.

ACKNOWLEDGMENTS

One of the chapters begins with a quote by Ralph Waldo Emerson: "Once you make a decision, the universe conspires to make it happen." I decided that I wanted to write a book that would be beneficial to those who read it in some important way. So I made my presence known, as so many aspiring authors do, through the Internet. Less than two weeks later, Steven Harris, a literary agent, found me.

I am grateful to him for not only expediting the arrangement that led to my writing this book, but also for his encouragement and support. Steve was thorough and patient as he explained the various aspects of the book publishing process, and was enthusiastic about my securing the opportunity to write this book. I truly enjoyed our interactions and look forward to further explorations with him in the future.

For all of Steven Harris's efforts, the book would never have happened if acquisitions editor Lara Asher hadn't believed in my ability to write about an idea she had actually conceived within her publishing house, Globe Pequot Press. Lara wanted a book to be written about making decisions that would benefit large groups of people, particularly women, whom she considered the target audience. She was an enthusiastic advocate, expedited my book contract, and served as my mentor for the project. She encouraged me, anticipating the reservations I might have and then dispelling them, as well as reacting to the results of my efforts with both surprise and delight. She scrutinized my offerings and led me on a path toward my goal.

During development of the book, the editorial reins were passed on to another individual who was most helpful in seeing the manuscript through to its point of acceptance. To that end, I am grateful to editorial director Mary Norris, at Globe Pequot Press, for her wisdom and insightful guidance.

Once accepted, the task at hand became converting the manuscript into a book. For this, my sincerest gratitude is extended to Ellen Urban, the project editor who expedited the work to its final form: a book on making decisions.

A special note of gratitude is extended to my mentor, Dr. Joseph Riggio, for enlightening me with his wisdom and insights; and for teaching me the Mythogenic Self™ Process, the foundation model for the suggestions offered in this book.

Finally, I wish to thank my parents, Dan and Sylvia Green, posthumously, for having bestowed their unique talents upon me. They were each exquisitely creative, talented people, particularly in the literary arts and music categories. I sincerely believe I inherited the capacity to write from both of them—and my unconventional sense of humor, from my father.

BIBLIOGRAPHY

Bandler, Richard, PhD. *Get the Life You Want.* Deerfield Beach, FL: Health Communications, Inc., 2008.

Bandler, Richard, and John Grinder. *Frogs into Princes: Neuro-Linguistic Programming.* Moab, UT: Real People Press, 1979.

Basler, Barbara. "Stress: Why It's Making You Sick," *AARP Bulletin* (May 2009).

Baumeister, R. F., E. Bratslavsky, C. Finkenauer, and K. D. Vohs. "Bad Is Stronger than Good," *Review of General Psychology,* 5, 323–370 (2001).

Campbell, Joseph. *The Hero with a Thousand Faces.* New York: Barnes & Noble Books, 1949.

Carrion, Victor, MD. "Severe Trauma Affects Kids' Brain Function," *Drug Trial News,* July 30, 2007.

Clippinger, John Henry. *A Crowd of One.* New York: Public Affairs (Perseus Book Group), 2007.

Feldenkrais, Moshe. *The Elusive Obvious.* Cupertino, CA: Meta Publications, 1981.

Fraser, Roye, and Ann M. Gardner, PhD. "Generative Imprinting™ and the Function Mode," *Anchor Point,* Vol. 5, No. 3 (March 1991).

Gatto, John Taylor. *Weapons of Mass Instruction: A Schoolteacher's Journey through the Dark World of Compulsory Schooling.* British Columbia, Canada: New Society Publishers, 2009.

Gladwell, Malcolm. *Blink: The Power of Thinking Without Thinking.* New York: Little, Brown & Co., 2005.

Hanna, Thomas. *The Body of Life.* Rochester, VT: Healing Arts Press, 1993.

Hanna, Thomas. *Somatics: Reawakening the Mind's Control of Movement, Flexibility, and Health.* Cambridge, MA: Da Capo Press (Perseus Book Group), 1988.

Hartmann, Thom. *Healing ADD: Simple Exercises that Will Change Your Daily Life.* Grass Valley, CA: Underwood Books, 1998.

Kahneman, Daniel, and Amos Tversky. "Prospect Theory: An Analysis of Decision under Risk," *Econometrica,* Vol. 47, No. 2 (March 1979).

Kammen, Rick, and Lee Norton, PhD. "The Client's Wounds: Trauma and Decision Making," *The Advocate,* Vol. 22, No. 2 (March 2000).

Kershaw, Sarah. "For Teenagers, Hello Means, 'How About a Hug?'" *The New York Times,* May 28, 2009.

Klein, Gary. *Sources of Power: How People Make Decisions.* Cambridge, MA: MIT Press, 1999.

Lynch, Dudley, and Paul L. Kordis. *Strategy of the Dolphin: Scoring a Win in a Chaotic World.* New York: William Morrow and Company, 1988.

Mason, John L., PhD. *The Guide to Stress Reduction* (2nd ed.). Berkeley, CA: Celestial Arts, 2001.

Merkin, Daphne. "A Journey Through Darkness," *The New York Times Magazine,* May 10, 2009.

Riggio, Joseph S., PhD. *Towards a Theory of Transpersonal Decision-Making in Human Systems* (PhD dissertation). Alexandria, VA: Bernelli University, 2005.

Rose-Charvet, Shelle. *Words that Change Minds.* Dubuque, IA: Kendall/Hunt Publishing Co., 1997.

Rozin, P., and E. B. Royzman. "Negativity Bias, Negativity Dominance, and Contagion," *Personality and Social Psychology Review,* Vol. 5, No. 4, 296–320 (2001).

Siegel, Daniel J., MD. *The Developing Mind.* New York: The Guilford Press, 1999.

Updegraff, J. A., R. C. Silver, and E. A. Holman. "Searching For and Finding Meaning in Collective Trauma: Results from a National Longitudinal Study of the 9/11 Terrorist Attacks," *Journal of Personality and Social Psychology, 95,* 709–722 (2008).

Wilson, Robert Anton. *Prometheus Rising.* Tempe, AZ: New Falcon Publications, 2004.

INDEX